African Mythology

*Captivating Myths of Gods, Goddesses, and
Legendary Creatures of Africa*

Free Bonus from Captivating History (Available for a Limited time)

Hi History Lovers!

Now you have a chance to join our exclusive history list so you can get your first history ebook for free as well as discounts and a potential to get more history books for free! Simply visit the link below to join.

Captivatinghistory.com/ebook

Also, make sure to follow us on Facebook, Twitter and Youtube by searching for Captivating History.

Contents

Introduction

The continent of Africa is home to fifty-four countries that together harbor over three thousand cultures, each with their own ways of life and each with their own stories. Some of these stories have their origins in the folk beliefs of people native to their particular region, while others were imported from or influenced by cultures from elsewhere who settled in Africa.

A great number of African folktales have been transmitted orally from person to person down through the ages, but since the nineteenth century, many stories have been written down and transmitted to audiences beyond the boundaries of the cultures that created them. One important—and tragic—conduit for the transmission of these stories beyond African shores was the European slave trade. Captured Africans who were brought to the Americas and the Caribbean fought to keep alive what they could of their home cultures, and this included their folktale traditions.

African folktales come in many different types. Some are myths explaining the origins of things, while others are tales of heroes with supernatural abilities. Animal stories are many and varied, and they usually involve some kind of trickster who uses his wiles to get out of sticky situations and sometimes into them. There are also cautionary tales explaining why it is important to behave well and treat others with respect, while other stories have a style and shape similar to that of a fairy tale.

This current collection presents ten stories, each taken from a different culture. As such, this book is but a small taste of the variety in the stories that African peoples have to tell and makes no claim to being in any way representative.

The first section of the book deals with the exploits of animal tricksters. Kwaku Anansi, the spider (Ghana); Nwampfundla, the hare (Mozambique; and the redoubtable Frog (Angola) all work either for themselves or for someone else, trying to get something of value from a powerful being while trying (and sometimes failing) to avoid consequences to themselves and others.

Hero tales fill the second section of the book. The first two stories, from Angola and South Africa, respectively, deal with male protagonists who, in the typical way of heroes, have supernatural births and supernatural abilities, who go out seeking adventure, and who struggle against monstrous beings that would seek to destroy them. The final story—also from South Africa—departs from the supernatural hero trope and instead presents the tale of an exceptionally observant and wise little girl who is able to save herself and her sister from a group of murderous men.

Stories from Kenya and Nigeria present moral lessons to be learned. These cautionary tales provide lessons about treating others with respect and about the dangers of greed.

The last two stories show the influence of Islam and Arab culture on African peoples. The first of these stories is from Eritrea and involves the character of Abunawas, an important Arab poet whose fictionalized persona became the hero of many folktales. The second is a fairy tale from Libya, which shows the influence of Arab storytelling in the way it resembles many of the tales in the *Arabian Nights* collection.

"African folklore" as an umbrella term is really quite inadequate as a description for the stories told by African peoples. Each of the stories in this book—and the thousands of others created and told by the myriad African cultures—is influenced by the traditions and religions practiced by their creators and by the environments in which those creators lived. These stories also represent living traditions of storytelling, traditions that have survived colonialist rapacity and the vicissitudes of modern society, and that still have new things to tell us every time we listen to them.

Part I: Animal Tricksters

How Spider Bought the Sky God's Stories *(Ashanti, Ghana)*

Kwaku Anansi, the spider, is the primary trickster in West African folklore. Stories about Anansi originated in Ghana, but when Ghanaian natives were taken abroad as slaves, the stories went with them, entering into the folklore of their descendants in the United States and the Caribbean.

The story about Anansi retold below has two particularly interesting features. One is the concept of the ownership of stories, which is common in many traditional societies. In these societies, if one wishes to tell a story owned by another person, one first must get permission to do so. Here, the stories all originally belonged to Nyankonpon, the Sky God, who asks a hefty and practically impossible price for them, but once Anansi meets the god's price, the stories become his.

The other feature is the role played by Anansi's wife, Aso. Most animal tricksters in other cultures tend to work alone: for example, Coyote in Indigenous North American lore, or Nwampfundla, the hare, in stories from the Ronga people, one of which is told below. In the story of how Anansi bought all the stories from the Sky God, Anansi relies on his wife's good advice to help him play the tricks necessary to get the items demanded by Nyankonpon, making the success of that project a team effort.

There was a time when all stories belonged to Nyankonpon, the Sky God. Kwaku Anansi, the spider, thought to himself, "It is not fair that the Sky God should have all the stories. I mean to see whether I can get them from him."

Anansi went up to Heaven. He went before Nyankonpon and said, "I want to buy all your stories. How much will I have to pay for you to sell them to me?"

Nyankonpon laughed and said, "Anansi, you are just one small creature. Many great men have tried to buy my stories. Whole cities of people have tried to buy my stories. No one has ever succeeded. What makes you think you will be able to meet my price?"

"Oh, I think I'll be able to meet it," said Anansi. "Just tell me what you want."

"Very well," said Nyankonpon. "If you want to buy my stories, you must bring me Onini, the python; Osebo, the leopard; Mmoatia, the fairy; and Mmoboro, the hornets. Bring me all of these things, and the stories will be yours."

Anansi went home and told his wife, Aso, that he had made a bargain with the Sky God to buy all his stories. "First I must bring him Onini, the python," said Anansi. "Have you any advice about how I should go about capturing him?"

"Oh, yes," said Aso. "This is what you must do: get the branch of a palm tree and some string creeper, and bring them down to the river."

"Ah! I know what to do now," said Anansi, and so he went out and got a long palm branch and some string creeper, and as he walked down to the river, he pretended to be having a conversation with his wife.

"He is not as long as this palm branch," Anansi said in his own voice.

"No, indeed," Anansi said in Aso's voice. "He is much longer than that."

"You lie," Anansi said in his own voice. "There is no way he is even this long."

As Anansi got closer to the river, Onini, the python, heard the conversation. He slithered over to Anansi and said, "What are you arguing about?"

"My wife and I had an argument about whether you are longer than this palm branch. She thinks you are longer, but I think she is wrong."

Onini said, "Bring the branch here, and we can measure to see who is right."

Anansi put the branch down on the ground, and Onini stretched himself out beside it. Quick as a wink, Anansi took the string creeper and tied Onini to the palm branch.

"Caught you!" said Anansi. "Now I shall bring you to the Sky God, and he will have to sell me all his stories."

Anansi brought the python up to Heaven and showed him to Nyankonpon. "Here is Onini, the python, the first part of my payment."

Nyankonpon looked at the python, who was tied to the palm branch. He reached out and touched the python and said, "I accept this as the first part of your payment. Bring me the rest, and my stories will be yours."

Anansi went home and told Aso how he had captured the python. "I think I shall capture the hornets next," said Anansi. "Have you any ideas about how I might do that?"

"Oh, yes," said Aso. "This is what you must do: find a gourd and a plantain leaf. Fill the gourd with water, and you may use those things to capture the hornets."

"Ah! I know what to do now," said Anansi, and he went out and found a gourd and a plantain leaf. He filled the gourd with water and then went looking for the hornets. Soon enough, he came upon a whole swarm of hornets. He took the plantain leaf and covered his head with it, then splashed the hornets with water from the gourd.

"Oh, dear, it is raining!" said Anansi to the hornets. "Would you like a place to shelter from the rain, Hornets? I have this nice plantain leaf, but I see you have no shelter. Come and sit inside my gourd until it is dry."

"Thank you!" said the hornets, and they all flew into the gourd. As soon as the last one had entered, Anansi plugged the mouth of the gourd. "Caught you!" he said. "Now I shall bring you to the Sky God, and he will have to sell me all his stories."

Anansi brought the hornets up to Heaven and showed them to Nyankonpon. "Here is Mmoboro, the hornets, the second part of my payment."

Nyankonpon looked at the gourd full of hornets. He reached out and touched the gourd and said, "I accept this as the second part of your payment. Bring me the rest, and my stories will be yours."

Anansi went home and told his wife how it had gone with the hornets. "Now I have to capture Osebo, the leopard," said Anansi. "You give me such good advice; what should I do to capture Osebo?"

"Go and dig a deep hole," said Aso.

"Yes! That is the very thing," said Anansi. "I know what to do now."

Anansi went out and looked for the leopard's tracks. When he found a place he thought a leopard was likely to visit, he dug a deep hole and covered it with banana and plantain leaves. Then he went home.

In the morning, Anansi went back to the hole. He looked over the lip of the hole and saw the leopard there.

"Help me!" cried the leopard. "Help me! I have fallen into this pit, and I can't get out again."

"Oh, you poor thing!" said Anansi. "That must be very wretched indeed for you."

"Indeed, it is," said the leopard. "Please, won't you help me get out?"

"I could do that," said Anansi, "but I bet you'll just eat me right up for my pains."

"No, no!" said the leopard. "I won't eat you, I promise! Just help me out of here, and I'll go my own way and you'll go yours."

"Very well, I'll help you," said Anansi.

Anansi got two long sticks and some string creeper. "Here, put your paws over these sticks, two in front and two in back," said Anansi. "Then I'll use the sticks to pull you up."

When the leopard put his paws over the sticks, Anansi tied them tightly with the creeper.

"Caught you!" said Anansi. "Now I can bring you to the Sky God, and he will have to sell me all his stories."

Anansi brought the leopard to Heaven and showed him to Nyankonpon. "Here is Osebo, the leopard, the third part of my payment."

Nyankonpon looked at the leopard, who was tied by his paws to the sticks. He reached out and touched the leopard and said, "I accept this as the third part of your payment. Bring me the rest, and my stories will be yours."

Anansi went home and told his wife how things had gone with the leopard. "Only one payment remains," said Anansi, "and I already know how I will get it. Please, Aso, will you make me some pounded yams?"

"Yes, I certainly will," said Aso, and off she went to cook the yams.

While Aso was busy preparing the yams, Anansi took some wood and carved an *akua*, a wooden doll with a flat face. He made it so that the head would move when pulled with a string. Then Anansi went to a tree and collected a great deal of sticky sap, which he spread all over the doll's body.

"My wife, are the yams ready?" said Anansi when the doll was done.

"Yes, they are," said Aso. "Come and take them."

Anansi took the yams Aso had made and put some of them into the hands of the doll. Then he took the doll to a tree where he knew fairies lived. Anansi hid himself in a nearby bush, with one hand holding onto the string connected to the doll's head. Sure enough, a fairy came along and saw the doll there with its hands full of delicious yams.

"Akua, may I share your yams with you?" said the fairy.

Anansi pulled the string, and the doll nodded its head.

"Thank you!" said the fairy. The fairy reached out her right hand to take the yams, but her hand stuck to the sap on the doll. Then she took her left hand and tried to remove the right one, but her left hand stuck as well. The fairy pushed at the doll with her right foot, but this was no help. It was stuck fast to the sap on the doll's body, and her left foot was stuck too as soon as she tried to use that one to remove the right foot.

When the fairy was completely stuck to the doll, Anansi came out from behind the tree and tied the fairy up. "Caught you!" said Anansi. "Now I can bring you to the Sky God, and he will have to sell me all his stories."

Anansi brought the fairy to Heaven and showed her to Nyankonpon. "Here is Mmoatia, the fairy, the fourth and last part of my payment."

Nyankonpon looked at the fairy, who was tied to the doll. He reached out and touched the fairy and said, "I accept this as the fourth and last part of your payment. You have done what many great men have failed to do. You have done what whole cities have failed to do. You have met my price, and now my stories are yours. From now on, whenever someone tells a story, they must say, 'This is Anansi's story.'"

And this is why all stories are Anansi stories and why all stories belong to the Spider.

Nwampfundla and the Elephant *(Ronga, Mozambique)*

This story about Nwampfundla, the hare, is retold from a set collected in the early twentieth century by the Reverend Herbert L. Bishop, a member of the South African Association for the Advancement of Science. Bishop recorded these stories as they were told to him by Samuel Mabika, who Bishop describes as "a great warrior [in his youth and] a man of considerable importance in his tribe."

Nwampfundla uses his tricksterish wiles to get things for himself that otherwise are forbidden and to make fools of creatures who are more powerful than he is. However, he does not get away completely scot-free; Nwampfundla often has to pay a price for his trickery.

In his notes to the stories he collected, Bishop states that the word "nwa" is used as the equivalent of "Mr." The name "Nwampfundla" therefore literally means "Mr. Hare."

As everyone knows, the lion is the great chief of all the animals. Every animal in the bush recognizes him as king. Even the elephant knows that the lion is chief, despite the elephant being much larger by far. Whenever the lion strolls by, all the animals say, "Hail, O Chief!" as he passes.

Like any good chief, the lion also has many servants and advisors to help him. One of these servants was Nwampfundla, the hare. Wherever the lion went, Nwampfundla went with him. Whatever the lion told Nwampfundla to do, he would do.

One day, the lion said, "I think we should go somewhere else. Come with me."

And so all the animals who were servants of the chief made ready to leave. They collected all their belongings and things they would need for the journey. When the lion said, "Let us go," all the animals went with him.

The animals walked along, following the lion. It was a great procession, for the lion had many, many servants. They walked and walked until they came to a place that had a tree full of delicious fruit. Since the day was almost over, some of the animals went to the lion and said, "O Chief, we should stop here for the night. Look, there is a tree full of delicious fruit. This would be a good place for us to stop and a good place for us to spend the night."

The lion looked at the tree. He said, "Yes, I agree. This is a good place to stop and spend the night. But the fruit of the tree is only for me. No one else is to eat it. The rest of you can look about for other things to eat, but this fruit is for me."

The animals put down the things they had been carrying. They spread out their sleeping mats and made ready to spend the night. But Nwampfundla went to the lion's chief advisors and said, "I would like to speak to you about something."

"Yes, we will listen, Nwampfundla," the advisors said.

"Well," said Nwampfundla, "I am concerned about this fruit tree, the one with the fruit that our chief said we are not to touch."

"What about it?"

"Well, I don't want to get into trouble because of it," said the hare. "If someone should go and steal all the fruit while the rest of us are sleeping, surely I will be accused. Everyone will say, 'That Nwampfundla, he thinks he can get away with anything, even stealing all the lion's fruit.'"

"Why should anyone say that?" said the advisors.

"Oh, I just have this thought that they might," said the hare. "But I know how we can prevent any trouble on my account. You know that big mortar we brought for stamping corn? I'll lie down here, and you can turn the mortar upside down on top of me. That way if the fruit goes missing, everyone will know that someone else did it because I will have been shut up in the mortar all night."

The advisors laughed, but they agreed to shut Nwampfundla up in the mortar. The hare lay down on the ground, and the advisors turned the mortar upside down on top of him. Soon the camp became quiet, and all the animals went to sleep.

Once the hare was certain all the others were sleeping, he cautiously lifted up one edge of the mortar and peeped out. He looked this way and that, and everywhere he looked he saw only sleeping animals. When he saw that everyone was asleep, he crawled out from under the mortar as quietly as he could. He went over a little way to where there was a basket. He stood listening, making sure no one had heard or seen him. When he felt safe, he picked up the basket, then stopped again to listen. But none of the other animals stirred because they had eaten so well of the fruit from the other trees that the lion said they could have.

Nwampfundla went over to the lion's special tree. Holding the basket, he began to climb. He went a little way, then stopped to listen. Then he went another little way, then stopped to listen. In this way, he went all the way up the trunk and into the branches where the fruit was. When he reached the fruit, he began to eat it, and every time he finished one of the fruits, he put the stone into his basket.

Having eaten his fill of the fruit, the hare climbed quietly down the tree. Then he went to where the elephant was sleeping and hung the basket full of fruit stones behind the elephant's ear. Then he went back over the mortar, climbed underneath it, and went to sleep.

In the morning, the animals awoke and stretched in the sun. They talked among themselves as they packed up their things, making ready to continue their journey. They heard a scratching sound from inside the overturned mortar, and the hare's voice coming faintly from inside it, saying, "Please let me out! The sun is up, and I want to see the light!"

"Oh, right," said one of the advisors. "I almost forgot we put the hare under that last night."

The advisor went over and let Nwampfundla out from under the mortar. After he yawned and stretched in the sunlight, Nwampfundla went over to the lion. "Good morning, O Chief!" he said. Then he looked over at the fruit tree and said, "Look at that! I told you it was true. I told you someone would eat all the fruit you said was yours. That's why I had your advisors put me under that big mortar during the night. I didn't want to be accused."

The lion looked at the tree and saw that all the fruit had indeed been eaten. "Who did this?" he roared. "Who disobeyed me and ate all my fruit?"

All the animals quaked in fear.

"Come here and stand before me," said the lion. "Tell me who did this."

The animals all came to stand before the lion, but no one could tell him who had eaten the fruit. Then the hare came and stood in front of the lion. "If it please you, O Chief," he said, "I propose a test to see which of us stole the fruit. May I tell you my test?"

"Yes," said the lion. "Tell me."

"Very well," said the hare, "but first you must tell the animals that they have to help me."

"You all heard what the hare said," said the lion, "and that is my command, that you help him. Now, hare, tell us your plan."

"Well, first we dig a big, long pit," said the hare, "and then everyone has to jump over it. That way we will discover who took the fruit."

The animals all helped to dig the pit, and when it was ready, Nwampfundla showed them where they should jump. The lion said, "I am the chief, so therefore I jump first."

The lion jumped over the pit. Nothing happened.

Then the hare jumped. Nothing happened.

Then the leopard jumped, and nothing happened. One by one, all the animals jumped over the pit, but they were still no closer to finding out who had taken the lion's fruit.

Finally it was the elephant's turn, and he was the last one left. He jumped over the pit, and when he landed on the other side, the basket of fruit fell down from behind his ear. All the fruit stones fell out of the basket and scattered on the ground.

Nwampfundla said, "Look! We have caught the thief! See? He had a basket full of the fruit stones. The elephant is the one who ate all that fruit."

"How could I have eaten all that fruit?" said the elephant. "Look at me. I can't climb trees at all. I didn't take that fruit, not one bit of it."

The animals didn't believe the elephant. Then Nwampfundla said, "Shame on you, for stealing the king's fruit."

The lion said, "Let the elephant be killed!"

The other animals fell upon the elephant and killed him. The king gave Nwampfundla a big piece of the elephant's flesh and told the hare to carry it. And so the animals all resumed their journey with their king, and Nwampfundla staggered along behind them, carrying a big piece of the elephant's flesh.

Now, the hare was a very small animal, and the piece of elephant's flesh that he carried was very big, and soon the hare became tired. He started lagging behind the other animals. Nwampfundla also was very sad because the elephant had been killed even though he had done nothing wrong.

Nwampfundla walked behind the other animals, crying and feeling sorry for himself and saying, "The elephant didn't eat any of the lion's fruit, but they killed him anyway."

The animals walking in front of the hare heard him crying. They heard him talking to himself, but they couldn't understand what he was saying.

Suddenly, the lion stopped. He turned around and saw Nwampfundla lagging behind all the other animals. The lion called to the hare and said, "Nwampfundla! Come up here and walk next to me. You are lagging too far behind."

"O my Chief," said the hare, "I want to do your bidding, but I must carry this heavy piece of meat. I am very small, and the piece of meat is very big. I cannot walk fast enough to be beside you and carry this piece of meat at the same time."

The lion had the piece of meat divided into two pieces. He told one of the larger animals to carry the big piece and gave the smaller piece to Nwampfundla. Then the lion and his entourage resumed their journey.

It was not long before Nwampfundla again was staggering along behind all the other animals, crying and talking to himself.

"Oh, it is such a sad thing that they killed the elephant. He didn't do anything wrong. He didn't eat any of the fruit. I'm the one that ate it, but he's the one that was killed."

Again the lion turned and saw Nwampfundla struggling along on the path, crying and talking to himself. The lion said, "Nwampfundla! Why do you stagger along so far behind everyone? You must come and walk closer to me."

Nwampfundla answered, "O my Chief, I want to do your bidding, but this piece of meat is too heavy for me since I am only a very small animal."

The lion took the piece of meat from the hare and gave it to another animal to carry. Then he gave his assegais, his bundle of javelins, to Nwampfundla, saying, "Here, you must carry my assegais. They are not too heavy. Also you must walk in front of me."

Nwampfundla took the assegais and walked in front of the lion. While he walked, he began singing the song that he had made about the elephant. "Oh, they killed the elephant, even though he did nothing wrong. They killed him, even though he ate none of the lion's fruit. They killed the elephant, but it was I who ate the fruit."

This time the lion heard what the hare was saying. "What is that you are singing about? Was it really you that ate all my fruit from my special tree?"

"Yes, I ate the fruit, my Chief, but the elephant paid the price for it, and I am very sorry about that."

Then the lion became very angry. "So, it was you the whole time!" He turned to the other animals and roared, "Catch that thief!"

Nwampfundla ran away as fast as his legs could carry him, with all the other animals chasing along behind. But no matter how fast the other animals ran, none of them could catch Nwampfundla. Soon the hare noticed a hole in the ground, so he dove into it. The animals saw him go in. They went back to the lion and said, "That rascal went down this hole. What shall we do with him now?"

"Find a way to get him out," said the lion.

The animals went into the bush and found a good, long stick. They cut the stick to have a hook at one end, then they took the stick back to the hole. They put the stick down the hole and began to fish around with it. The hook caught Nwampfundla by the leg, but the hare only laughed and said, "Well, aren't you clever, putting a stick down the hole and catching only a root! You'll never get me that way!"

The animals took the stick out of the hole and put it down again, and this time it hooked itself around a root. When Nwampfundla saw that the stick was hooked on a root, he began to cry and scream. "Oh, no! You have hooked me by the leg! What will I do now?"

All the animals thought they had caught Nwampfundla for sure. They pulled and pulled on the stick, but it would not budge. The lion came and helped too, and again they pulled. They all pulled as hard as they could, and finally the root broke, sending all the animals falling backward on top of one another.

The lion was enraged. "You scoundrel! You rascal! When I catch you, I will have you skinned and chopped up for my dinner!"

Then the lion turned to the other animals and told them to try again. The animals put the stick down the hole, and the hook caught on the hare's leg. But when the hare laughed, the animals thought, "We must have caught another root. Surely the hare would not laugh if we had hooked him."

The animals removed the stick from the hole, then put it down again. This time they hooked another root, and Nwampfundla began to cry and beg for mercy. "Aha!" said the animals. "This time we've really got him." They pulled and pulled and pulled on the root until it broke, sending all the animals falling backward on top of one another.

The lion was even more angry than before that the hare had tricked them yet again. He roared out all the terrible things he wanted to do when he finally caught the hare, and his anger was so great that all the animals were very much afraid of him. But Nwampfundla sat in his hole, listening to the lion rage on and on, laughing and saying, "Yes, you do go on about what you will do to me, but first you have to catch me! And you cannot do that, for I, Nwampfundla the hare, am the greatest of all the animals!"

Finally, the lion and the other animals got tired of listening to the hare laugh at them. "Fine," said the lion. "If he thinks he's so great for having gone down that hole, he can stay there forever. Find grass, and plug up this end of the hole. Make it so that he cannot get out. That will teach him to make sport of me."

The animals did as the lion bid them. They took a great quantity of grass and shoved it into the hole. They packed the grass in very tightly, so that the hare could not get out. Then the lion and the other animals resumed their journey.

When the animals had gone, Nwampfundla went to the grass and tried to pull it away so that he could get out. He pulled and he pulled and he pulled, but no matter what he did, the grass stuck fast. The animals had packed it in so tightly that there was no way the hare could remove it. He was stuck inside that hole for good.

Nwampfundla sat inside the hole feeling very sorry for himself. After a while, he began to feel hungry. He got hungrier and hungrier, until at last he ate one of his own ears. This satisfied him for a time, but after a while, he became hungry again. He tried to ignore the hunger, but at last it was too strong, so he ate one of his own legs.

More time passed, and soon Nwampfundla found himself becoming thirsty. He tried and tried not to think about it, but finally he took one of his eyes out and ate it, thinking to quench his thirst with the tears that were inside it.

After Nwampfundla had eaten his ear, his leg, and his eye, there came a great storm with much wind. The wind blew so strongly that it blew the grass plug out of the hole. When the storm passed, Nwampfundla realized he could see the opening of the hole. He crept very carefully up to the entrance, and he looked around. There was no one to be seen, so he crept out of the hole.

In a nearby tree, there was a beehive. Nwampfundla took some of the wax and used it to fashion two little horns. He stuck the horns on his head and limped off to the lion's home.

The king saw the hare come into the kraal, the fenced village where the lion lived with his servants and advisors. The lion asked the other animals who this stranger was. "Oh, that must be Nwampfundla, the hare," said the animals, "the one who gave you so much trouble."

"Nonsense," said the hare. "Did this Nwampfundla have only one ear? Did he have only three legs? Did he have only one eye? Did he have horns on top of his head?"

The animals all had to admit that Nwampfundla did not have those things.

"Well, of course he didn't," said the hare. "How could he? I am a special hare from a special society of hares. We all have one ear, one eye, three legs, and horns on our heads, and there are precious few of us. You are privileged to have seen me at all, for I can run faster with three legs than any other animal can run with four, and I see farther and hear better than animals with two eyes and two ears. I am the best servant any chief could ever wish for."

The lion was very pleased by what the hare had said. "If you really can do all those things," said the lion, "then please stay on and be my servant. A chief needs servants who can do such marvelous things as you can."

And so it was that Nwampfundla once again became a servant to the lion.

The Daughter of the Sun and Moon *(Ambundu, Angola)*

Na Kimanaueze is an important culture hero of the Ambundu people of Angola. He is the subject of a cycle of hero stories and a character in hero stories about his son and grandson. The stories originally were transmitted orally, but they were first recorded in writing by European anthropologists in the nineteenth century.

In this story, the younger Kimanaueze wants to marry the daughter of the Sun and Moon, and although he is a major character and the person around whom the story revolves, he himself does not do the work of securing the young woman's hand in marriage. That task falls to the trickster Frog, who finds a way to go back and forth between Heaven and Earth and to convince the Sun and Moon that their daughter should be the younger Kimanaueze's bride.

We see in this story some important aspects of Ambundu culture surrounding courtship and marriage. The younger Kimanaueze must prove that he is worthy to marry the young woman by paying an appropriate bride-price, and with each installment that Frog brings up to Heaven, the young woman's family provides a good meal for their guest, not realizing that it is Frog and not the suitor who has been visiting their home.

The great hero and chieftain Na Kimanaueze had a son named Kimanaueze kia Tumb' a Ndala. When the son of Na Kimanaueze had grown to manhood, his father came to him and said, "It is time we found a wife for you. There are many beautiful girls in our village. Choose one, and we will go to her family and ask whether you might marry her."

But the son of Na Kimanaueze said, "I will not marry any of the girls in our village."

"Very well," said Na Kimanaueze. "Perhaps we can go to the next village and find a wife for you there."

"No, that will not do either," said the son of Na Kimanaueze.

"Do you wish to look for a bride among the people of a different country?" said Na Kimanaueze.

"No," said the son of Na Kimanaueze. "I do not want a bride from a different country."

"Who then will you marry?" said Na Kimanaueze.

"I will marry the daughter of the Sun and the Moon," said the son of Na Kimanaueze.

Na Kimanaueze did not know what to say at first. "You have great ambitions, my son, and I'm not sure they are realistic. How do you think you will be able to win that girl for a wife?"

"I don't know," said the son of Na Kimanaueze, "but I'm sure I'll find a solution some way."

Na Kimanaueze did not know what he could do to persuade his son to give up this silly idea, so he left his son to it, thinking that once he failed, he would come to his senses and marry a nice girl from their own village.

The son of Na Kimanaueze, for his part, thought and thought about how to go about asking for the hand of the daughter of the Sun and Moon. He decided that the best thing to do would be to write a letter asking her parents to let her be his bride. He thought very carefully about what to say, then wrote a respectful letter to the Sun and Moon and sealed it.

"Now to get it up to Heaven," said the son of Na Kimanaueze, and so he walked out of the village to see whether he could find someone to act as his messenger. The son of Na Kimanaueze came across a deer. "Hello, Deer," said the son of Na Kimanaueze. "Can you take a message to the Sun and Moon for me, please?"

"Oh, my!" said Deer. "I can't do that at all."

Then the son of Na Kimanaueze went to Antelope and said, "Hello, Antelope. Can you take a message to the Sun and Moon for me, please?"

"No," said Antelope. "I don't even know how to do that."

The son of Na Kimanaueze continued on his journey until he came across a hawk. "Hello, Hawk," said the son of Na Kimanaueze. "Can you take a message to the Sun and Moon for me, please?"

"I can fly very high and very well," said Hawk, "but I don't think I could get up far enough to deliver your message.

Next the son of Na Kimanaueze spoke with Vulture, but Vulture had the same answer as all the other animals. "I can't do that," said Vulture. "I tried once, but I couldn't fly high enough."

The son of Na Kimanaueze was very discouraged. He had asked all the animals he met whether they could be his messenger, and every single one told him no. The son of Na Kimanaueze sat down on the banks of a river to rest. He was very sad and despaired that his letter would ever be delivered.

Frog saw the son of Na Kimanaueze sitting there. Frog went to the son of Na Kimanaueze and said, "Why are you so sad?"

"I am sad because I want to marry the daughter of the Sun and the Moon, but I have no way to deliver my letter to them asking for her hand. I asked Deer and Antelope and Hawk and Vulture to help me, and many other animals besides, but they all said no."

"Oh!" said Frog. "Never fear; I think I can help you."

The son of Na Kimanaueze scoffed. "Hawk and Vulture said they couldn't do it, and they fly in the sky all day. How could a frog possibly hope to get into Heaven and bring my letter to the Sun and the Moon?"

"It is true that I cannot fly," said Frog, "but I know where the servants of the Sun and the Moon go to fetch water. I am not a flying animal, but I am a water animal, and if you entrust your letter to me, I will see it delivered, on my honor."

The son of Na Kimanaueze handed the letter to Frog. "Very well, I will trust you. But if it turns out that you have been lying to me, things will go very badly for you."

"I understand," said Frog, and then he hopped away with the son of Na Kimanaueze's letter in his mouth.

Frog hopped all the way to the well where the servants of the Sun and the Moon came to draw water. He made sure that no one was watching and then slipped into the water. He found a good place to hide and settled in to wait. Not long afterward, the servants came to the well and began putting their jugs into the well to draw water. Frog waited until just the right moment, then hopped into one of the jugs before anyone could see him.

When the servants had filled all their jugs, they went back up into Heaven using the webs that Spider had spun for them, and put the jugs in their proper places. Frog waited until the sounds of footsteps and voices faded, then he crawled out of the jug. Frog looked about the room and noticed that a table stood in the very middle. He hopped onto the table, left the letter there, then hopped down and found a place to hide and wait.

Frog didn't have to wait long. The Sun came into the room, thinking to drink some water, and he saw the letter with his name and his wife's name on the outside. He thought it very odd that a letter to him should be in the room where the water was kept. The Sun called all the servants together. He showed them the letter and asked, "Where did this letter come from?" But none of the servants knew.

The Sun opened the letter and read it. The letter said, "I, Kimanaueze kia Tumb' a Ndala, son of the chief Na Kimanaueze, respectfully ask the hand of the daughter of the Sun and Moon in marriage."

The Sun was very surprised. Why would a mortal man want to marry his daughter, and more importantly, how had a mortal man managed to deliver the letter all the way to Heaven without the Sun knowing about it? Then the Sun left the room, not saying anything to anyone about what was in the letter.

When Frog saw that it was safe, he jumped back into one of the jugs. When it was time to refill the jugs, the servants went down Spider's web and took all the jugs to the well, including the one Frog was in. The servants lowered the jugs into the water, and Frog jumped out without anyone seeing him.

Frog then went to the son of Na Kimanaueze and said, "I did it! I delivered your message to the Sun. He has read it, but I don't know what his reply will be."

"You are lying!" said the son of Na Kimanaueze. "You lie to me. You just hid that letter somewhere, and now you are pretending you went up to Heaven. Things will go very badly for you now."

"Wait!" said Frog. "Please trust me. Wait a while, and see whether the Sun answers you."

Six days passed with no answer from the Sun and the Moon. The son of Na Kimanaueze wrote another letter that said, "I, Kimanaueze kia Tumb' a Ndala, son of the chief Kimanaueze, wrote to you asking for your daughter's hand in marriage. It has been six days now, and I have received neither a yes nor a no from you." The son of Na Kimanaueze gave the letter to Frog and said, "Take this new letter up to Heaven, and see to it that you return with an answer this time."

Frog took the letter in his mouth and hopped over to the well. He hid in the well, and when the servants of the Sun and Moon came to get water, Frog jumped into one of the jugs. He waited until the servants had gone back up to Heaven on Spider's web, the jug had been put in its place, and the water room was empty before he jumped out and put the letter on the table. That done, he went to his hiding place.

Again the Sun came into the room to get a drink, and again he saw a letter on the table. The Sun asked the servants, "Has someone been giving you letters to bring to me?" But the servants all said no.

The Sun then wrote a reply to the son of Na Kimanaueze. The reply said, "I consent to let you marry my daughter on one condition: you must come to Heaven in person with your first bride-gift. I wish to meet you and know what kind of a man my daughter will be marrying." The Sun left the letter on the table and went out of the room.

When Frog thought it was safe, he came out of his hiding place and jumped up on the table. He picked up the Sun's letter and went to hide in one of the water jugs. In the morning, the servants picked up the jugs to refill them at the well, and Frog jumped out when his jug was lowered into the water. Then he went in search of the son of Na Kimanaueze to bring him the Sun's reply.

Frog went to the son of Na Kimanaueze's house with the letter and knocked on the door. From inside, the son of Na Kimanaueze said, "Who is there?"

"It is Frog, and I bring you the Sun's reply."

The son of Na Kimanaueze opened the door and saw Frog sitting there in front of the door, with a letter in his mouth. The son of Na Kimanaueze took the letter, and Frog hopped away to do his own business.

The son of Na Kimanaueze read the letter. He went to his chest and took out forty gold pieces. He put the gold into a bag and wrote another letter to the Sun. The letter said, "Here are forty gold pieces for the first gift. I have brought them as you asked. I wait to hear what you would consider a fair bride-price."

In the morning, the son of Na Kimanaueze went to the river. There he found Frog and said to him, "Please take this bag of money and this letter to Heaven."

Frog hopped away with the money and the letter. He went to the well and waited for the servants to take him up to Heaven in one of the jugs. When the water room was empty, Frog left the money and the letter on the table, then hid himself and waited.

The Sun came into the room and saw the bag and the letter on the table. He opened the bag and read the letter. He smiled and then went to show his wife, the Moon, what the son of Na Kimanaueze had sent.

"See, my wife? This suitor sends us a fine first present, and he is a chief's son to boot. I think he will make a fine husband for our daughter."

"Oh, yes," said the Moon. "I think we should let him marry her. I think we should make him a meal to eat while he is here."

The Moon called the servants and told them, "Roast a hen, and make other good things to eat. Then leave the platter on the table in the water room." When the meal was cooked, the servants took it and put it on the table, then they left. Frog came out of his hiding place and ate the meal, then went back to hide once more.

After a time, the Sun came back into the room and saw that the meal had been eaten. He wrote another letter and left it on the table. The letter said, "You have brought a fine first gift. My wife and I are pleased. Your bride-price shall be a large sack of gold coins."

Frog picked up the letter once it was safe and hopped back into one of the jugs. When he arrived back on Earth, he went to the son of Na Kimanaueze, gave him the Sun's reply, then went back to tend to his own business at the river.

The son of Na Kimanaueze read the letter and was very pleased to see the Sun's reply. He gathered up coins and put them into a large sack. Then he wrote a letter that said, "Here is the bride-price you requested. Soon I will write to you again to set the day for your daughter to become my bride."

In the morning, the son of Na Kimanaueze gave the letter and the sack of gold to Frog to take up to Heaven. Frog went up in one of the jugs, waited until the water room was empty, then left the gold and the letter on the table. He hopped over to his hiding place to wait, and soon thereafter the Sun and the Moon came to see what their daughter's suitor had left them. They saw the large sack of gold and read the son of Na Kimanaueze's letter, and they were both very pleased indeed. The Moon called her servants and told them, "Roast a young pig for our new son-in-law, and leave it here on the table."

The servants killed and roasted the pig. They put it on a platter and left it in the water room, then they went away. Frog jumped up on the table and ate all of the pig. Then he jumped back into one of the jugs and waited to be taken back down to Earth, where he jumped back into the well and waited for the servants to be gone.

Frog hopped away to the son of Na Kimanaueze's house. He knocked on the door, and when the son of Na Kimanaueze opened it, Frog said, "They have accepted your bride-price. Now you have to set the date for your wedding."

Now the son of Na Kimanaueze had a new problem. He couldn't send Frog up to Heaven to bring his bride down; surely Frog was too small for such a burden. But how to fetch the daughter of the Sun and the Moon down to Earth? The son of Na Kimanaueze went and asked all the large animals he could think of who might be able to go up to Heaven and bring his bride back down, but every animal said that they wouldn't be able to do that.

The son of Na Kimanaueze went back to the riverbank to sit and think. Frog saw him there and asked, "What is troubling you?"

"I cannot find anyone to bring my bride down from Heaven."

"Let me do that," said Frog.

"Oh, Frog, that is a very kind offer," said the son of Na Kimanaueze, "but surely you're too small for such a burden. Besides, I don't think I should ask you to do anything else for me; you've already helped me so very much, I hate to ask yet another thing from you."

"Never fear," said Frog. "I am very small, but I am also very clever, and I will bring your bride down to Earth for you."

"Thank you, my friend," said the son of Na Kimanaueze. "I will wait as patiently as I can for you to return with her."

Frog hopped away to the well to wait to be taken up to Heaven. When he arrived, he went to his favorite hiding place and waited until night fell. After many hours, the Sun went to bed, and everything was dark and quiet. Frog came out of his hiding place and hopped to the bedroom of the daughter of the Sun and Moon. He hopped onto the young woman's bed and took out her eyes. He wrapped the eyes securely in a clean cloth and then went back to his hiding place to sleep until morning.

Morning came. The Sun got up, and the servants began to go about their business. But there was something wrong; the daughter of the Sun and the Moon usually arose when her father did, but this morning she was nowhere to be found. A servant was sent to see whether she was well or not. The servant found her still in her bed, weeping.

"Why do you not get up?" said the servant.

"I do not get up because something is wrong with my eyes," said the young woman. "I cannot see."

The servant told the Sun and the Moon what was wrong with their daughter. They went to her chamber and asked, "What is wrong, my daughter?"

"Something is wrong with my eyes. I cannot see anything at all," she said.

The Sun called for messengers. When they arrived, the Sun said, "Go down to Earth. Find the witch doctor Ngombo. See whether he can tell us what is wrong with our daughter."

The messengers went to the house of Ngombo. When they arrived, they said, "We are here to ask your advice."

Ngombo went into his house and came back out with the things he needed to learn what needed to be done and why the messengers were there. Ngombo sat down upon the ground and cast his divining objects. He looked at them closely, then said, "You have come to ask me about someone who has an illness in their eyes. This person is a woman. Also, you were sent here to me; you did not come because you wanted to. Have I said true?"

"Yes," said the messengers. "Everything you said is true."

Then Ngombo cast his divining objects again. He looked at them closely, then said, "The woman who has an illness in her eyes is betrothed, but the wedding has not yet happened. Her husband-to-be says, 'I am the one that made the woman blind. Send her down to me. If you do not, she will die.' You must bring the woman to her husband as soon as may be. I have spoken my judgment. You must do as I have told you."

The messengers returned to Heaven and told the Sun everything that Ngombo had said. "Very well," said the Sun. "We will bring her down tomorrow."

In the morning, Frog returned to Earth in one of the water jugs. He went to the son of Na Kimanaueze's house and said, "You shall wed your bride this very day."

"I think you are lying, clever Frog," said the son of Na Kimanaueze. "I do not see her here."

"She will be here by sunset," said Frog. "Just you wait."

While Frog was returning to Earth in a jug, the Sun went to Spider and said, "I need to send my daughter down to her husband today. Can you weave a web strong enough to take her down safely?"

"Oh, yes," said Spider. "I will have it done before the end of the day."

Spider set to spinning a great web. She spun and spun and spun her silk. It took her almost all day, but finally it was ready.

Toward the end of the day, Frog went back to the well to wait. As the sun was starting to set, the Sun's servants took his daughter to Earth on the special web Spider had made for her. They brought her to the well where they fetched their water, then went back up to Heaven.

When Frog saw that the young woman was standing next to the well, he said, "Never fear! I am here to take you to your husband and to heal your eyes."

Frog gave the young woman back her eyes, then led her to the son of Na Kimanaueze's house. Frog knocked on the door, and when the son of Na Kimanaueze answered, Frog said, "Here indeed is your bride, the daughter of the Sun and the Moon."

The two young people looked upon each other and were very pleased. Soon the wedding was held, with much celebration, and the son of Na Kimanaueze and the daughter of the Sun and the Moon lived a long and happy life together.

Part II: Hero Tales

The Twin Brothers *(Cabinda Province, Angola)*

Cabinda is a province of Angola that sits outside the boundaries of that country. Cabinda is bordered instead by the Democratic Republic of the Congo to the south and east and by the Republic of the Congo to the north.

The story of the twin brothers told here is typical of the hero tale. We have two brothers, Mavungu and Lembe, who display remarkable growth and who have extraordinary powers. Here the powers are contained in a charm or fetish with which each boy is born and with which they can work all kinds of magic.

The story retold below follows a common arc: one brother heads off to seek his fortune, and when he does not return, the other goes looking for him. The search is successful, but unlike many other stories of this type, it does not end well; this story concludes with a violent twist.

Once there was a woman who was with child. When her time came to be delivered, her labor was very long and very difficult, but in the end she gave birth to two twin boys. The woman named the boys Mavungu and Lembe. Mavungu was the first to be born, and Lembe followed after.

Now, these boys were no ordinary children. They each were born with a valuable charm, and they each were nearly fully grown at birth. And so it was that Mavungu decided soon after he was born that he would set out on his travels.

At that time, the daughter of Nzambi, the creator of all things, was of an age to be married. The leopard went to Nzambi and said, "I would like the hand of your daughter in marriage."

Nzambi replied, "You will have to ask her consent first. It is up to her to decide who she will have for a husband."

The leopard went to Nzambi's daughter and asked her to marry him. She refused, and so the leopard went home, feeling very sad indeed.

Other animals came to offer themselves as husbands for Nzambi's daughter: the gazelle, the wild boar, and every other animal that had breath. One by one they asked for the young woman's hand, and one by one she refused them.

Mavungu soon learned that the daughter of Nzambi was receiving suitors. He decided that he would win her for his wife. Mavungu took his charm and asked it to help him in his quest. Then he took up many blades of grass, and with the help of the charm, he transformed them into different things that he could use on his journey. One blade of grass became a knife; another became a horse. In this way he transformed all the blades of grass until he felt he had everything he needed, and when this was done, he set out on his journey.

Mavungu traveled on and on. He went many, many miles, traveling all through the morning and well into the afternoon, until finally he became faint from hunger. He took out his charm and said to it, "Are you planning to let me starve?" In the blink of an eye, the charm set a delicious feast out for Mavungu. Mavungu ate and was happy and satisfied.

When he was done, Mavungu said, "O charm, it is not right that all these dishes should be left here on the ground for any passerby to take. Make them disappear." And so the charm made everything disappear.

Mavungu resumed his journey. Soon the sun began to set. Mavungu said to his charm, "I will need a place to sleep for the night," and so the charm prepared a good sleeping place for Mavungu where he could rest in comfort and safety until the morning.

When the sun rose, Mavungu told the charm to clear away his sleeping place and then resumed his journey. He journeyed on and on for many days, and for many more days after that, until finally he came to Nzambi's town. Nzambi's daughter happened to catch sight of him approaching, and she immediately fell in love with him. She ran to her father and mother and said, "I have seen the man who I will marry. I love him, and if I cannot marry him, my life will be over."

Mavungu made his way through the town and finally arrived at Nzambi's house, and there he spoke to Nzambi. "I have heard that your daughter is to be married," said Mavungu. "I offer myself to be her husband."

"Go and speak to her," said Nzambi. "If she consents, then you may marry her."

Mavungu went to speak to Nzambi's daughter, and when they first set eyes upon one another, they realized they loved one another. They embraced and then ran to tell the young woman's parents that they would like to be wed. And so it was that Mavungu and his bride were taken to a beautiful house, where they slept together while all the rest of the town danced and sang and feasted far into the night.

In the morning, Mavungu woke and noticed that the house contained a great many mirrors, every single one of which was covered by a cloth. Mavungu woke his bride and said, "Why are all these mirrors covered? I would like to see myself in one of them. Can you uncover it?"

"Certainly," said the young woman. She lifted the cloth of one of the mirrors, but when Mavungu looked into it, he saw not himself but the town in which he was born.

"Show me another," said Mavungu, and so the young woman unveiled that mirror too. In that mirror, Mavungu saw another town that he knew. The young woman unveiled mirror after mirror, and in each one Mavungu saw a place that he had been before.

Finally, there remained but one veiled mirror. "Unveil that one, too," said Mavungu.

"I dare not," said his bride.

"Why?" said Mavungu.

"Because that is a town from which no one has ever yet returned. If you but catch a glimpse of it, I know you will want to go there, and if you go, you will never come home to me."

"Even so, I wish to see it," said Mavungu.

The young woman refused even more strongly, but Mavungu kept asking her until finally she relented. When the veil was lifted from the mirror, Mavungu looked into it and saw a very horrible place that surely was the most dangerous town in the whole world.

Mavungu said, "That is a place I must go."

"No! Please don't go there!" said the young woman. "You will never come back to me, and I cannot live without you!"

But no matter how the young woman pleaded, and no matter how many tears she shed, Mavungu was steadfast in his resolve. He gathered up his things, mounted his horse, and set out in search of the horrible town from which no one had ever returned.

After many days on the road, Mavungu finally came to the outskirts of the town. There he saw an old woman sitting next to a fire.

"Greetings, Mother," said Mavungu. "May I have a bit of your fire to light my pipe?"

"Certainly," said the old woman. "Tie up your horse tightly, then come closer and take some for yourself."

Mavungu dismounted, tied up his horse tightly, then walked over to where the old woman was sitting. But when he had come near enough, the old woman killed him, and then she killed his horse.

Now, back in Mavungu's hometown, his twin brother, Lembe, became concerned, because he had not heard from Mavungu for a terribly long time. Lembe took his charm and a handful of grass, and using his charm, he transformed the grass into all the things he would need on his journey. One blade of grass became a knife, another became a horse, and so on until he had all the things he would need. Then Lembe set out in search of his brother.

After many days' travel, Lembe finally arrived at Nzambi's town. Nzambi caught sight of him and ran out to greet him. "Mavungu!" said Nzambi. "You've come home at last!"

"I am not Mavungu," said Lembe. "I am his brother, Lembe."

"Nonsense," said Nzambi. "I know who you are. You are my son-in-law, and now that you are home, we shall have a great feast!"

And so the feast was prepared, and everyone in the village rejoiced, especially Nzambi's daughter. She was so happy she could not stop dancing and singing, and she kept calling Lembe by his brother's name. No matter how often or how strongly Lembe protested, the young woman refused to believe that Lembe was not her husband.

When the sun set and the feast was over, Nzambi's daughter led Lembe to the house she shared with her husband. Lembe refused Nzambi's embraces, saying, "I am too tired from my journey. Perhaps another time." Nzambi's daughter was disappointed, but she did not protest. When she was fast asleep, Lembe told his charm to prepare a separate chamber for the young woman. The charm did as Lembe bid, and so Nzambi's daughter slept in one place and Lembe slept in another. In the morning, the charm let Nzambi's daughter out, so she did not know that she had not slept with Lembe.

In the morning, Lembe noticed that the house was all full of mirrors covered with cloths. As his brother had done before him, Lembe asked Nzambi's daughter to remove the veils and let him see the mirrors. She removed the veils one by one until the only one left was the mirror that showed the terrible town. Nzambi's daughter refused at first to remove the veil from that mirror, but finally she gave in to Lembe's insistence and let him see it. As soon as Lembe looked into the mirror, he knew where his brother had gone.

Lembe prepared to go and find his brother, but when Nzambi found out what he was doing, he said, "Please don't leave. That is a terrible place you are going to. Nobody ever comes back alive. Think of my daughter, your young wife. You are barely married, and the whole time you were gone, she pined and grieved."

Lembe said, "Yes, I know, and I am sorry for her distress, but I must go on this journey. And you needn't fear: I already came back from there once, so surely I shall come back a second time."

And so Lembe set out on his journey, and after many days' travel, he came to the outskirts of the town. There he saw the old woman sitting next to her fire. "Greetings, Mother," said Lembe. "May I have a bit of your fire with which to light my pipe?"

"Certainly," said the old woman. "Tie your horse up tightly, then come and get some for yourself."

Lembe dismounted, but when he tied up his horse, he only did so loosely. Then he headed over to the fire, and when he got to where the old woman was sitting, he killed her. When the old woman was dead, Lembe looked for his brother's bones and the bones of his horse. Soon enough, he found them, and when he had put them all in order, he touched them with his charm. Mavungu and his horse came back to life again.

Mavungu and Lembe rejoiced to see one another again, and when they were done greeting one another, they looked for the bones of all the people the old woman had killed and brought them back to life.

Then they set off on the journey back to Nzambi's town, with all the resurrected people following them.

On the way back to Nzambi's town, Lembe explained what had happened while he was there, how everyone kept insisting that he was Mavungu, and how Lembe had made sure that he and his brother's wife had slept separately. Mavungu was very grateful that his brother had been so thoughtful.

They journeyed on for a little while, then Lembe said, "What shall we do about all our followers?"

"I think I should be their leader because I am the eldest," said Mavungu.

"Yes, but it was I who brought you back to life," said Lembe. "Surely that counts for something."

The brothers argued and argued, and finally Mavungu became so angry that he killed his brother. Mavungu and his followers resumed their journey, but Lembe's horse stayed behind with Lembe's body. When the others were well out of sight, the horse took Lembe's charm and touched it to his body. Lembe came back to life again. Then he mounted his horse and went in search of his brother.

Meanwhile, Mavungu arrived home with all his followers. Nzambi and the rest of the town rejoiced greatly to see that he had returned safely, but none rejoiced more than Mavungu's wife. As before, Nzambi commanded a great feast be held to celebrate Mavungu's safe return.

In the middle of the festivities, Lembe arrived. He went up to Mavungu and killed him. The townspeople were horrified, but Lembe explained what had happened, and the people agreed that Lembe had acted correctly.

The Tale of Uthlakanyana *(Zulu, South Africa)*

Uthlakanyana is the trickster hero of a series of Zulu tales, two of which are retold below. Like many tricksters and heroes,

Uthlakanyana has a miraculous origin and exhibits superhuman powers starting from the day he is born. He begins showing his tricksterish side right at the beginning, first fooling all of the men of the village by tricking them out of their meat, then by fooling his mother by eating the birds she had cooked while she was still asleep, then convincing her that she had cooked them so long only the heads were left. The second story also revolves around cooking and food, but this time the victims of Uthlakanyana's cleverness is a family of cannibals. Uthlakanyana tricks the cannibal mother into getting herself boiled to death and then tricks her sons into eating her.

To Western readers, Uthlakanyana's treatment of his own mother might seem odd at best and callous at worst, but in a note to his retelling of the tale, author Henry Callaway says that this likely is an attempt on Uthlakanyana's part to give himself a reasonable excuse for leaving, without which he cannot cut ties with his mother to go out into the world by himself.

The Birth of Uthlakanyana

There once was a woman who was expecting a child. When the time grew near for her to be delivered, she heard a small voice say, "Mother! Give birth to me now! The people are eating all of my father's cattle!"

"What is this?" thought the mother. "It is not time for my child to be born, and an infant cannot speak. I must be hearing things."

But again the voice came, saying, "Mother! Give birth to me now! The people are eating all of my father's cattle!"

The woman went to her husband, who was the king of the village and who was in the kraal slaughtering some cattle. The woman told her husband what had happened. The people there also heard what the woman said. "Let us hear what the child says!" said the people.

"Yes!" said the father. "Let us all be silent so that we might hear the child together."

Everyone held very still and waited. Soon the voice came from the mother's womb, saying, "Mother! Give birth to me now! The people are eating all of my father's cattle, and I have not yet had my share!"

All the people agreed that this was a very wondrous thing. Then the father said, "All of you should go to your own homes. My wife will go into our home and give birth now."

Everyone left the house, and the woman gave birth to the child. When the woman saw her child, she was quite astonished, for although he was very small, he looked like an old man and could already stand and walk by himself. The child went to the place where the men were sitting around a fire eating meat. When the men saw the creature approach, they became afraid and ran away, for the creature was small like an infant but looked like an old man. The child paid the men no heed. He simply took a piece of meat that the men had cooked, then sat down by the fire and began to eat.

The men then went to the mother of the child and said, "That creature there eating meat by our fire: is that the child who spoke within you and to whom you have just given birth?"

"Yes, indeed it is," said the mother.

The men marveled at this. "This is a wonder that has been wrought for us. Surely you are a queen, and this child is to be a great one among us."

The child heard what the men and his mother said about him, so he went to his father and said, "Father, I know that you and the others think that I am but a child, but I am not. I wish you to hold a test that will prove that I am a man full grown. Gather all the men and boys of the village into the kraal. Then take the whole haunch of an ox, and throw it outside the kraal. At your word, all the men and boys will try to be the first to get the haunch and take it back into the kraal. Whoever does this will be known as a man for certain."

The father agreed that it was well to do this, so he gathered all the men and boys into the kraal. Then he took the haunch of an ox and threw it outside the kraal. At the father's word, all the men and boys surged toward the gate of the kraal, pushing and shoving each other, trying to be the first to go through the gate and thus be the first to seize the haunch. But the child stayed away from the mass of bodies and instead crawled beneath the bars of the kraal. He ran over to the haunch, picked it up, raised it over his head, and then brought it to his mother to cook before the first of the men and boys finally managed to escape through the gate.

When the child arrived at his mother's house with the ox's haunch, he said to her, "Mother, here is the meat I have brought you."

His mother replied, "This is a good day, and I am very happy because my child is a very wise man."

The child then went back to the kraal, where his father was butchering a steer and giving meat to the men of the village. The father was about to give a piece of meat to one of the men when the child walked up and said, "Give me that meat. I shall put it in your house for you."

"Certainly," said the man.

"Thank you," said the child.

The child took the meat and went into the man's house. He took some of the blood from the meat and smeared it onto the storage mat and hanging stick, then brought the meat to his mother's house. When that was done, the child returned to the kraal, where his father was about to give a piece of meat to another man.

"Give me that meat," said the child. "I shall put it in your house for you."

"Certainly," said the man.

"Thank you," said the child.

As he had done with the first man's portion, the child took the meat and smeared some blood on the man's storage mat and hanging stick, but then brought the meat to his own mother's house. In this way, the child took the meat meant for each man of the village but brought it to his own mother instead.

When the men went into their houses, they saw that the storage mats and hanging sticks all had blood on them but that the meat was nowhere to be found, for every last piece had been taken to the house of the child's mother. The men went to the child and said, "We gave you our meat, and you said you would put it in our houses. There is blood on the storage mat as though it had been laid there and on the hanging stick as though it had been used to hang the meat, but we cannot find the meat anywhere. What have you done with our meat?" But the child would give them no answer other than that the meat was in their houses and that the blood on the utensils testified to that.

The women of the village had watched what had happened all day. When they saw the confusion of their men, they all said, "Do you not understand? This child is Uthlakanyana. Have you not seen that although he has the stature of a child, he walks and talks and behaves like a man? Have you not understood that he has tricked you well today, not once, but many times? Surely he was not begotten in the usual way. Surely the king of our village is not his father. This child is different and wondrous. He spoke while he was yet in the womb, and he has bested every man in this village on the very day he was but newly born. He will surely do many great things."

Uthlakanyana and the Cannibal

One day, Uthlakanyana went down to the river to hunt. While he was looking for prey, he came across a great many bird traps. Each one of them had a bird in it. Some traps even had two or three! Uthlakanyana took all the birds from the traps and brought them home to his mother.

"Mother, please take this heavy load from me," he said.

"What load is it you carry, my son?" said his mother.

"I caught a great many birds when I went out hunting today, and I am weary from carrying them all."

The mother took the birds from her son and marveled at how many he had caught. "My son is a man full grown, and a wise one, too!" she said. "Look at this fine catch of birds he brings to me!"

"Cook all of them, Mother," said the child. "Put them in a pot, and seal it well with cow dung. Set it over the fire overnight, and I will eat them in the morning. But for tonight, I shall be sleeping elsewhere. I shall go to the house where all the other boys sleep." And with that, the child went out of his mother's house and went to the house where all the boys slept together.

When the child arrived at the house where the boys were sleeping, they all said to him, "Get out! We don't want you here."

"Why?" said the child. "I am a boy and so should be allowed to sleep here with you, who are all boys yourselves. What, do you think I am a girl?"

"No," said the boys, "but we do not trust you. You took all the meat that belonged to our fathers, the meat that the king had given them. And we know that the king is not really your father."

"Is that so?" said the child. "Who is my father, then?"

"Oh, we have no idea," the boys replied, "but you are some kind of wonder-child, that is for sure, and likely will get up to some kind of mischief if we let you sleep here."

"All right, then," said the child, "I was thinking of leaving, but since you're making a fight out of this, I will stay and sleep here just to spite you."

The boys scoffed. "You couldn't fight us if you tried. You might be very clever with words, but you were just born yesterday, and you don't have the strength to best us. But you are very clever with words, and neither we nor our fathers can best you in that way." And then the boys turned their backs to the child and went to sleep. Soon Uthlakanyana went to sleep, too.

In the morning, Uthlakanyana went back to his mother's house. There he found his mother was still sleeping. Uthlakanyana unsealed the pot where the birds were cooking and found that they were ready to eat. He ate the bodies but left the heads behind. Then he went outside and got some cow dung. He put it in the bottom of the pot and placed the bird heads on top of it. After he did this, he sealed the pot up again, just like it had been before he ate the birds, and during all of this, his mother slept on.

Uthlakanyana left his mother's house. He walked a little way into the village, then turned around and went back. He stopped outside the door to his mother's house and said, "Mother! I am here! Open the door, please!" His mother opened the door for him, and he went into her house.

"Oh, I am so very hungry, and it's already so late in the morning," said Uthlakanyana. "Surely you have slept too much. Those birds have probably turned all to dung inside the pot for having been left there so long."

Uthlakanyana unsealed the pot and opened the lid. "Look! I was right! They're all turned to dung."

"How did this happen?" said his mother.

"I know how it happened, even if you don't," said Uthlakanyana. "I am a grown man, but you are a small child. I spoke to you when I was yet in the womb, telling you to give birth to me. I am older than you, so very, very old. And you are not my mother, and your husband, the king, is not my father. It pleased me to be born from you, but now it is time for me to leave. I must go traveling all about, but you and your husband must stay here and live together."

The mother took the bird heads and the cow dung out of the pot. "Truly you spoke when you said the bodies would be turned to dung," she said.

"Let me see them," said Uthlakanyana, and when she showed the bird heads to him, he took them and ate them all. Then he said to his mother, "You ate up all my birds, so I have eaten all the heads." Then Uthlakanyana took up his staff and left his mother's house and started off on his travels, muttering the whole time about how angry he was that his mother had eaten all the birds herself and left him nothing but the heads.

Uthlakanyana walked and walked, and then he came upon a place where many bird traps had been set. The traps each had birds in them, and so Uthlakanyana took them, thinking that they would make a fine meal later on. But the traps belonged to a wicked cannibal, and no sooner had Uthlakanyana removed the last bird from the traps than the cannibal grabbed him and shouted, "Why are you taking my birds from my traps?"

"Oh, please, please don't hurt me," said Uthlakanyana, dropping all the birds. "I didn't take anything! Please let me go!"

But the cannibal was very clever; he had smeared the traps with birdlime, and Uthlakanyana had some of it on his hands. "You did indeed take my birds," said the cannibal, "for I see your hands are smeared with the birdlime I put on the traps to catch thieves such as yourself."

"Please let me go!" said Uthlakanyana. "Please don't hurt me. Take me home to your mother. On the way we can clean off the birdlime, and if you treat me well, I will cook up nicely. Take me home to your mother, and she can cook me for your dinner. But you must leave the house while I am cooking because otherwise the dish will spoil and will not be worth eating."

"Very well," said the cannibal, and so he picked up the birds Uthlakanyana had dropped and took him to his mother's house. When they arrived, the cannibal said to his mother, "Look at this little thief I caught stealing from my traps. He says that he will cook up nicely but that I need to leave the house while he is in the pot. It's already late in the day, and I am tired. Cook him tomorrow morning after I have left the house." Then the cannibal and his mother gave Uthlakanyana a place to sleep, and they went to their own beds.

In the morning, the cannibal said to his mother, "Mother, cook up my little thief. Cook him well so that I will have a tasty dinner when I come home." Then the cannibal went out.

Uthlakanyana said to the cannibal's mother, "I will be more tender and tastier if you put me on the roof to dry out a bit in the sun before you cook me. You can go back to bed until I'm well dried. I'll call you when I'm done."

"Very well," said the cannibal's mother, and so she put Uthlakanyana on the roof of the house and went back to bed.

Now, this was a very clever thing Uthlakanyana had done, for from the roof of the house he could see which way the cannibal had gone. The cannibal walked a little way away from the house, where he met his brother, and together they walked away and went over the rise of a hill.

When the cannibal and his brother were gone, Uthlakanyana came down from the roof and went into the house. "I'm all dried," he said. "Let's start cooking. I know a game that we can play that will make me into the tastiest dish your son has ever eaten. I will show you how to play. We will need the biggest pot you have, for when I am all boiled, I shall swell up, and we don't want the pot to boil over."

The mother got her biggest pot, filled it with water, then set it over the fire. When that was done, Uthlakanyana said, "Here is how we play. First, I boil myself a little bit, then I get out of the pot. Then you climb in and boil yourself a little bit. Then we trade places."

After waiting for the water to warm a bit, Uthlakanyana took the lid off the pot and tested the water with his hand. "Oh, yes," he said, "that is hot enough to start cooking me."

The cannibal's mother took Uthlakanyana and put him in the pot, then sealed the pot with a lid. After a little while, Uthlakanyana said, "It's time for your turn! Take me out, please."

When Uthlakanyana was out of the pot, he looked at the fire. "Oh, dear. That will never do. We must build up the fire a bit." And so he built up the fire until it was roaring well under the pot, and the water was beginning to steam and bubble. "Look!" he said, "That means it's ready for you. Take off all your clothes and get in. It's quite warm and lovely in there."

When the cannibal's mother was undressed, Uthlakanyana put her in the pot and covered it with a lid. Soon the mother began to cry out from inside the pot. "Oh, help! Let me out! I am boiled to death! Let me out!"

"How can you say you are already boiled to death?" said Uthlakanyana. "If you were dead, you wouldn't be able to talk. No, I don't believe you. You must finish your turn in the pot, just as I finished mine."

After a little while, Uthlakanyana said to the mother, "Hey, there! Are you boiled yet?" But there was no reply from the pot, so Uthlakanyana said, "Ah, she must be well boiled now, because she doesn't answer me."

Then Uthlakanyana put on the cannibal's mother's clothes, and his body grew until it fit the garments perfectly. He lay down on the mother's bed and waited for her son to come home. Soon enough, the cannibal and his brother returned. "Hello, Mother," the cannibal said. "Is that little thief cooked nicely and ready to eat?"

"Oh, yes," said Uthlakanyana, pretending to be the cannibal's mother. "He cooked up very nicely. He even expanded quite a bit in the pot, so there's even more meat there than I thought there would be. You and your brother help yourselves; I've already eaten my share, and it was very good indeed."

The cannibals opened the pot and took out an arm. "Wait," said the cannibal's brother. "This looks an awful lot like Mother's arm."

"You shouldn't say that," said the cannibal. "You're going to bring a curse down upon Mother."

"I'm sorry," said the brother. "I take it back."

And so they ate the arm.

When the arm was gone, they reached into the pot and took out a leg. The cannibal's brother looked at the foot and said, "Doesn't this look an awful lot like Mother's foot? But I suppose I shouldn't say that, since I don't want to bring down a curse upon her."

Pretending to be the cannibals' mother, Uthlakanyana said, "Please don't worry; I'm over here, safe and sound. It's just the little thief who is in the pot." Then he got up and went to the door of the house. "I'm going out for a little while," he said. "You two boys finish your dinner. There's plenty there!"

The cannibal reached into the pot and drew out the other leg. He looked very closely at the foot and said, "Wait. This looks an awful lot like Mother's foot."

Uthlakanyana, meanwhile, walked quickly away from the house, and when he came to a place where he thought the cannibals might not be able to see him, he took off the mother's clothing and ran as fast as he could. When he had run far enough that he knew the cannibals would never be able to catch up to him, he turned and shouted, "Hey, cannibals! That was your mother's arm, and those were your mother's legs. You two fools have eaten your own mother!"

The cannibals heard Uthlakanyana and ran after him. "I told you that was our mother's hand and that was our mother's foot," said the brother as they ran. "I told you so, but you wouldn't listen."

Uthlakanyana ran until he came to the banks of a river. He knew the cannibals were chasing him, but the river was too deep to ford and too swift to swim, so he changed himself into a stick. Not long afterward, the cannibals arrived. "Now where has that little thief got to? said the cannibal.

"I think he must have crossed the river," said the brother. "See, here are his footprints on the bank."

The cannibal picked up the stick and threw it across the river in anger. But when the stick landed on the other side, it turned back into Uthlakanyana. "Thank you for throwing me across!" he said, and then ran away. The two cannibals stood on their side of the river, watching him go, and feeling very foolish indeed that they had been tricked that way. Then they went home, and Uthlakanyana continued on his own travels.

The Little Wise Woman *(Khoekhoe, South Africa)*

The Khoekhoe live in southwestern Africa and traditionally follow a nomadic pastoralist lifestyle. Formerly, these people were often referred to as "Hottentots," but that word has derogatory connotations. The term "Khoekhoe" used here refers to various Khoe-speaking peoples in Southern Africa.

The tale of the "little wise woman" retold below participates in the trope of the disadvantaged person who has special powers or insights that the advantaged people around them do not have. Both the little girl, who is the main protagonist, and the one-eyed man, who is the main antagonist, are disadvantaged in some way, the little girl by her age and size, and the one-eyed man by his half-blind state. Each of them uses their abilities to try to gain advantage, and each of them is ignored by the people around them who see them as lesser, to their own detriment. The only exception is the little girl's elder sister, who defends her younger sister and is willing to listen and follow instructions. In this way, she avoids the tragic fate of the other girls who treated the little wise woman dismissively.

The item of clothing called a kaross *mentioned in the story is made from animal hide with the wool or hair still attached. It is stitched together into a sleeveless jacket and is traditionally worn by the Khoekhoe people.*

A girl once set out to look for onions. She arrived at a place where she knew she could find some and found that a group of men had already arrived there before her. One of the men had only a single eye. The girl bent down to dig up the onions, and the men helped her. When her sack was full, the men said, "Why don't you go home and invite your friends to join you? There are plenty of onions for everyone."

The girl returned home and told all her friends about the onion field, but made no mention of the men. In the morning, the girls all picked up their sacks and set out to the onion field, with a little girl following after them.

"Why don't you tell your little sister to go home?" said one of the girls to the small one's elder sister. "She really shouldn't be coming with us."

"She's able to run by herself," said the elder sister. "It's not like any of us will need to carry her. Let her follow along."

When they arrived at the onion field, the little girl looked at the ground and saw there were many, many footprints. This made her uneasy. She went to the girl who had been there the day before and asked, "Why are there so many footprints? Weren't you alone last time?"

"Oh, those must be all mine," said the older girl. "I was walking around a lot, after all."

The little one didn't say anything else, keeping her suspicions to herself. She was a wise little woman and so kept looking about her while she worked. One time, she looked about and saw an anteater's hole.

The little one went back to digging onions, but kept looking up from time to time. She discovered that there were men close by, but she gave no sign that she had seen them, and the men seemingly could not see her.

When the little one had stopped working to look around yet again, one of the older girls said, "Why do you keep doing that? Just dig onions like the rest of us."

The little girl didn't reply, but she didn't stop looking either. After a little while, she stood up to look again, and she saw a group of men coming toward the field. One of them was the one-eyed man, and he was playing on a reed pipe. The little girl listened closely and discovered she could understand what the pipe was saying. Over and over, the reed pipe sang:

There will be blood, today blood will flow

There will be blood, today blood will flow

The girls heard the music of the reed pipe and began to dance. The little girl asked the older ones whether they could understand what the reed pipe was saying, but they all told her to stop asking silly questions. The little girl then started dancing with the others, but she made her way over to where her elder sister was dancing and tied her sister's *kaross* to her own, and they kept dancing together like that as the other girls became merrier and merrier. Soon the other girls were making so much noise and having so much fun that the two sisters thought they could slip away undetected.

As they walked away from the onion field, the little girl asked her sister, "Do you understand what the reed pipe is saying?"

"No, I don't," said the elder.

"It is saying, 'There will be blood, today blood will flow,' over and over."

Now, the little sister was truly a wise woman. She had her elder sister walk in front while she walked behind. The little girl stepped into her elder sister's footprints, which made it look like there was only one set of tracks, but she walked backward, so it wasn't possible to tell which direction they were going. The two girls walked like this until they came to the anteater's hole, where they climbed inside to hide.

After a little while, they heard the girls who were still in the field crying and screaming. The men had begun killing them, one after the other. The two sisters who had escaped heard the crying, and the elder one began to weep herself in grief for her friends. The little one said to her, "Be glad you came with me; if you had stayed, you would be dead just like all the others."

Back in the onion field, the men finished killing all the girls. The one-eyed man looked about and said, "Wait. There are two missing."

The other men said, "How would you even know that? You only have one eye."

"I do know," said the one-eyed man. "There are two others. We should go look for them."

The other men agreed to help look, and soon they found a single set of footprints outside the field. They couldn't decide whether these were the footprints of someone leaving or someone entering the field, but they decided to follow them out of the field anyway. Soon they came to the anteater's hole. They looked inside but didn't see anything. Then the one-eyed man looked. "They're in there!" he said.

The others laughed at him. "How would you even know that? You only have one eye."

"I do know," said the one-eyed man. "Look again, and you'll see them there."

The others looked again, but they still saw nothing, for the girls had hidden themselves behind a mass of cobwebs.

"I'll test whether there's really anyone in there," said one of the men. He took his assegai and thrust it into the hole. The tip of the assegai cut the elder sister's foot and it began to bleed, but before the man could pull the assegai out of the hole, the little sister wiped all the blood off. Then she said to her sister, "Don't cry or they will hear us."

When the assegai came back without any blood on it, the one-eyed man peered into the hole again. This time the little girl stared right back at him. The one-eyed man said to his companions, "I swear to you they are both inside that hole." But the other men jeered and said, "How would you even know that? You only have one eye."

The day had grown very hot, and the men became thirsty. They said to the one-eyed man, "We are going to get something to drink. You stay here and keep watch. You can get your drink when we come back."

The girls heard the other men leave, and when they were sure that the one-eyed man was alone, they began to sing a spell to him.

You dirty son of your father

Are you not thirsty as well?

You dirty son of your father

Dirty child of your father

Do you not also want to drink?

The one-eyed man fell under their spell. He said, "I'm too thirsty to wait for the others to come back," and then he left to get a drink for himself.

When the girls were sure the one-eyed man had gone, they crawled out of the hole. The little sister took her big sister on her back, and in this way they began to journey home. The way they had to go was across a plain that was flat and without trees, so when the men finished their drink and resumed looking for the girls, they saw them there in the distance. "There they go!" shouted the men, and they began to run after the girls.

The girls saw the men running toward them, so they turned themselves into thorn bushes. The beads the girls were wearing became drops of gum. The men arrived at the thorn bushes. They pulled the gum drops off the bushes and ate it. Then they lay down on the ground and went to sleep.

While the men were sleeping, the girls took the gum and smeared it on the eyes of the men, sealing them shut. Then the girls resumed their journey home.

When the girls had almost reached their kraal, the men woke up and found their eyes had been sealed shut with gum. "Oh, you layabouts!" said the one-eyed man. "You fell asleep and let the girls get away!"

"It's not like you're any better," said the men. "You fell asleep too, and your one eye is sealed shut just like our two eyes are."

The men removed the gum from their eyes and resumed looking for the girls, but they discovered that the girls had arrived safely at their parents' house, and so the men returned to their own village.

The girls told their parents what had happened and explained to the other villagers what had become of their daughters. The whole village wept and was in mourning but no one dared return to the onion field, not even to fetch the bodies of their daughters.

Part III: Cautionary Tales

The City Where People are Mended *(Hausa, Nigeria and Niger)*

The Hausa people are the most numerous of all African cultures, and the Hausa language is the most widely spoken, second only to Arabic. Primarily located in the Sahel and savannah regions of what are now Niger and Nigeria, Hausa communities are also found in neighboring states such as Cameroon, Chad, and Ghana, with others as far away as Eritrea. The Hausa people have embraced Islam since the Middle Ages, and many of their cities became important centers for trade along traditional African and Middle Eastern caravan routes.

The story retold below participates in several tropes common to folktales in many cultures. One such trope is the contrast between the good mother and the bad one, which goes hand in glove with the trope of the beautiful and ugly daughters. One twist on the latter, however, is that rather than being an antagonist in her own right—as she is in many other tales—the ugly daughter here is an innocent victim of her mother's own jealousy and greed. Jealousy and greed contrasted with generosity and mercy form the last trope, and also turn this story into a cautionary tale about treating others with respect.

The story mentions several types of food. One of these is fura, *balls of dough made of millet flour. The other is the fruit of the* adduwa *tree, which is similar to dates, although not as sweet.*

One day, the girls of the village decided to go into the forest to pick herbs. While they were in the forest, a great storm blew up from the east, sending down sheets and sheets of rain. The girls all ran to take shelter beneath a baobab tree, but when they found the tree was hollow, they went inside. No sooner had the girls entered the tree than the Devil came and closed it up behind them.

"Oh, please let us out!" cried the girls.

"No, I won't let you out," said the Devil, "not unless you give me your necklace and your clothes."

The girls handed the Devil their necklaces and clothes, except for one girl who refused. The ones who gave the Devil their things were let go, but the Devil kept the other one inside the tree. The girls who escaped ran to their friend's mother and told her everything that had happened and that the Devil still held the woman's daughter captive inside the baobab tree.

"Take me to the tree that I may know which one it is," said the mother. The girls led her to the tree, and the mother saw that there was a hole in the top that led down inside the trunk. The mother went home and cooked a meal for her daughter, then returned to the tree.

"Daughter!" she called. "I am here! I have food for you! Stretch your hand through the hole in the trunk, and I will give you your meal."

The girl heard her mother's voice, and so she put her hand through the hole in the trunk and received the food her mother had prepared. Once the girl had eaten all her food, the mother went home.

Now, there happened to be a hyena skulking nearby, and he saw and heard everything that went on. Thinking to take advantage of the situation, he went over to the tree and said, "Daughter! I am here! I have food for you! Stretch your hand through the hole in the trunk, and I will give you your meal."

The girl heard the hyena calling to her from outside the tree. She did not recognize the hyena's gruff voice. "You are not my mother," the girl said. "Go away."

The hyena went to a blacksmith's shop. "Change my voice so that I sound like a human," said the hyena.

"Very well," said the blacksmith, "but likely you'll eat the first thing you find in the road and that will undo all my work."

The blacksmith changed the hyena's voice, and the hyena trotted off on his way back to the tree. Along the road, the hyena came across a centipede. "Never pass up a free meal!" said the hyena, and he gobbled up the centipede in one bite.

Soon the hyena arrived at the baobab tree. "Daughter!" he called. "I am here! I have food for you! Stretch your hand through the hole in the trunk, and I will give you your meal."

But the hyena's voice was gruff and scratchy from having eaten the centipede, so the girl did not recognize it. "You are not my mother," the girl said. "Go away."

The hyena ran back to the blacksmith's shop in a fury. "You said you changed my voice, but it didn't work! I should gobble you up right where you stand!"

"Wait!" said the blacksmith. "Did you eat anything after I changed it the first time?"

"Well, yes," said the hyena. "There was a fat centipede in the road, and I was in the mood for a snack."

"That's why your voice changed back," said the blacksmith. "I'll fix it for you again; just don't eat me, and don't eat anything else yourself until after you've used the human voice."

The hyena went back to the baobab tree, this time taking care not to eat anything on the way. He arrived at the tree and called out, "Daughter! I am here! I have food for you! Stretch your hand through the hole in the trunk, and I will give you your meal."

This time the girl was fooled. She thought it was her mother calling to her, so she put her hand up through the hole in the tree. No sooner had she done this than the hyena jumped up and grabbed the girl's hand. He pulled the girl out of the tree and ate her on the spot, leaving only the bones behind, and then he went away.

When evening came, the girl's mother returned to the tree to give food to her daughter, and there she saw her daughter's bones lying on the ground. The mother wailed to find the dead body of her child. Then she went home to get a basket. She returned to the tree and tenderly collected all the bones. When she had every last bone, she set off to find the city where people were mended.

The mother traveled a long way down the road until she came to a place where food was cooking itself over a fire. "Food, can you tell me how to get to the city where people are mended?" asked the mother.

"Won't you eat me? Please, have a bite!" said the food.

"How can I eat when my daughter is dead? I will not eat you," said the mother.

"Very well," said the food. "Go down that road until you come to the place where it splits right and left. Take the right-hand road, and leave the one on the left behind."

The woman thanked the food and went down the road. On and on she walked until she came to a place where meat was roasting itself over a fire. "Meat, can you tell me how to get to the city where people are mended?" asked the mother.

"Won't you eat me? Please, have a bite!" said the meat.

"How can I eat when my daughter is dead? I will not eat you," said the mother.

"Very well," said the meat. "Go down that road until you come to the place where it splits right and left. Take the right-hand road, and leave the one on the left behind."

Again the woman walked down the road until she came to a pot where *fura* was being mixed. "*Fura*, can you tell me how to get to the city where people are mended?" asked the mother.

"Won't you eat me? Please, have a bite!" said the *fura*.

"How can I eat when my daughter is dead? I will not eat you," said the mother.

"Very well," said the *fura*. "Go down that road until you come to the place where it splits right and left. Take the right-hand road, and leave the one on the left behind."

The woman continued her journey, following the directions she had been given, and soon she arrived at the city where people were mended. She entered the city, and the people asked, "Why are you here?"

"I am here because the hyena ate my daughter, and I wish her to be mended," said the woman.

"Do you have all her bones?" asked the people.

"Yes, they are here in this basket."

"We will mend your daughter tomorrow," said the people.

The people gave the woman a place to sleep, and in the morning, they said, "Please go out and tend our cattle."

The woman went to the byre and let the cattle out into the pasture. Now, the food of these cattle was the fruit of the *adduwa* tree. The woman went to the tree and picked off all the ripe fruit and fed it to the cattle. Then she took some of the unripe fruit for herself and ate it. The woman fed the cattle ripe *adduwa* fruit all day, and at sunset, she brought them home and put them in their byre. No sooner had they reached the byre than the biggest bull started singing,

This woman is a good woman

She fed us ripe fruit all day

And kept none for herself

This woman is a good woman

Mend her daughter well!

The people heard the bull's song. They said to the woman, "Go into that hut and sleep well. Your daughter will be given back to you in the morning."

Sure enough, when the woman awoke in the morning, the people gave her her daughter back. The mother and daughter greeted one another with great joy, and then they went home together.

Now, the mother was not the only wife in that household. There was another wife, who was jealous because her daughter was ugly whereas the first wife's daughter was beautiful. The second wife saw the first one return with her beautiful daughter restored, and when the second wife had heard the tale of what happened, she began to scheme about how she might get her daughter restored as well. Maybe she might even become beautiful afterward!

The second wife called her daughter to her, and threw her into a large mortar. Then the second wife began to pound her daughter with the pestle. "No, mother! Do not kill me!" pleaded her daughter. But the second wife did not stop. She pounded her daughter until she was dead, and then she collected all the bones in a basket and set out for the city where people were mended.

The second wife traveled a long way along the road until she came to the place where food was cooking itself. "Food, can you tell me how to get to the city where people are mended?" said the second wife.

"Won't you eat me? Please, have a bite!" said the food.

The second wife looked at the good food and said, "You don't have to ask twice," and then she ate up all the food.

When the food was all gone, the second wife resumed her journey. On and on she walked until she came to the place where meat was roasting itself. "Meat, can you tell me how to get to the city where people are mended?" said the second wife.

"Won't you eat me? Please, have a bite!" said the meat.

The second wife looked at the good meat and said, "You don't have to ask twice," and then she ate up all the meat.

Again the second wife walked down the road until she came to a pot where *fura* was being mixed. "*Fura*, can you tell me how to get to the city where people are mended?" asked the mother.

"Won't you eat me? Please, have a bite!" said the *fura*.

The second wife looked at the good *fura* and said, "You don't have to ask twice," and then she ate up all the *fura*.

Once all the fura was gone, the second wife resumed her journey. After much walking, she arrived at the city where people were mended. The people of the city saw the second wife enter with her basket and asked, "Why are you here?"

The second wife said, "Oh, it is a very sad tale. A hyena ate my daughter, and I have brought her here to be mended."

"Do you have all the bones?" said the people.

"I do; they are in this basket."

The people took the basket and said, "We will mend your daughter tomorrow." Then they showed the second wife to a place where she could sleep for the night.

In the morning, the people told the second wife, "Please look after our cattle today."

"Very well," said the second wife, and she let the cattle out of their byre and took them out into the pasture. When the second wife got to the orchard of *adduwa* trees, she picked all the green fruit and gave it to the cattle while eating all the ripe fruit herself. The second wife fed the cattle on green *adduwa* fruit all day and then brought them home at sunset. No sooner had they reached the byre than the biggest bull started singing.

This woman is a bad woman

She fed us green fruit all day

And ate all the ripe fruit herself

This woman is a bad woman

Mend her daughter badly!

The people heard the bull's song. They said to the second wife, "Go into that hut and sleep until morning. We will bring you your daughter at sunrise."

The second wife went into the hut and slept, and in the morning, the people brought her daughter to her. But what a horror she was! One half of her nose was missing, and one arm, and one leg. Half of everything was missing!

The second wife hid her disgust and started on the road home with her daughter. But as soon as they were out of sight of the city, the second wife shouted, "You are not my child!" and ran away.

The second wife tried to hide in some tall grass, but her daughter followed her. When the daughter found her mother, she said, "Come, Mother, let us go home."

But the second wife said, "You are not my child! Leave me alone!"

The daughter replied, "Yes, I am your child, but you are not my mother."

Again the second wife ran away. She ran all the way home, and when she got to her hut, she went inside and closed and barred the door. Eventually her daughter arrived and said, "Open, Mother! I have returned home."

The second wife refused to open the door or even to speak to her daughter. The daughter said again, "Open, Mother! I have returned home."

This time the second wife opened the door. The daughter lived with her mother, and for the rest of her days, the second wife had to deal with the shame of having a disfigured daughter while the first wife's daughter was beautiful.

The Woman and the Children of the Sycamore Tree *(Maasai, Kenya)*

The Maasai of Kenya are known as fierce warriors and cattle rustlers. They live primarily on the meat and milk produced by their cattle, and are one of the largest groups of people living in Kenya. Their traditional lifestyle is nomadic, but in modern times, encroachment on their lands by towns and cities, as well as government prohibitions against living or grazing on protected lands, has forced many of them to settle in villages and give up many of their traditional ways.

In the cautionary tale about the dangers of ingratitude and anger retold below, one of the characters is the Maasai laibon, *or medicine man. The* laibon *has an important place in Maasai culture, functioning as a shaman, healer, and diviner who can give advice to those who need it. The story also centers on the fruit of the sycamore fig, a tree that has been cultivated in the Middle East and Sub-Saharan Africa since ancient times.*

There once was a woman who had lived a long and difficult life. She was very sad because her life had been so hard. She wondered whether perhaps life had been hard for her because she had never married and had never had any children. "I know what I will do," she said to herself. "I will go and ask the laibon to give me a husband and some children. Maybe then my life will be better."

The woman walked all the long way to the laibon's place. When she arrived, the laibon said, "What is it you want of me?"

The woman said, "I have had a long and difficult life. I think it is because I never married and never had children. Can you give me a husband and some children, please?"

The laibon thought for a few moments, then said, "I can give you either a husband or some children. I cannot give you both. You must choose."

"Oh!" said the woman. "I was hoping for both, but if I can only have one, then I would like some children."

"Very well," said the laibon. "If you would like to get some children, you must listen carefully to my instructions and follow them closely. First you must return home and gather up all your cooking pots. You must have at least three, but if you can carry more, that will be even better. Go into the forest and look for a sycamore that is bearing fruit. Fill the pots with as much fruit as they will hold, then put the pots in your house. When all the pots are filled and put away, then you must leave your house and go for a walk. Do not return until sunset."

The woman thanked the laibon and returned home. She gathered up her cooking pots, filled them with sycamore fruit, and put them away in her house. Then she went for a walk. She walked and walked until the sun began to set. She returned home, and as she approached her house, she heard the sound of children's voices. Her home was an astonishing sight. The kraal had been swept clean, the cattle taken out to pasture, the house tidied, and a meal was cooking on the fire. A crowd of children of all ages greeted her. "Mother! Mother!" they cried. "We are so glad you are home. See? We cleaned the house and the kraal, and the boys are out with the cattle. They will bring them home presently."

The woman was overjoyed that she had so many fine children. She lived with them very happily for many days. Then one day, the children did something to displease the woman. Nobody remembers what it was the children did, but everyone remembers what happened afterward. The woman began to scold the children. She said to them, "Oh, you are worthless children! You are nothing but children I got from a sycamore tree! Why should I have expected anything better from a bunch of tree-children?"

The children didn't answer her. They just stood there looking very sad indeed. Then the woman left the house. She went to visit some friends and spent the day with them. While the woman was gone, the children returned to the sycamore tree, where they turned back into fruit.

The woman returned home and saw that her house was empty. She called and called for the children, but they did not answer. A pang of fear went through her body. She ran to the laibon's house and said, "My children have all disappeared! If I put the sycamore fruit into the pots again, will they come back?"

The laibon said, "I don't know. Maybe you should go back to the tree and see whether it tells you what to do."

The woman thanked the laibon and ran home to get her cooking pots. Then she ran into the forest. She ran and ran until she came to the sycamore tree that had given her children before. She climbed up into the tree to pick the fruit that was hanging there, but the skin of every fruit she picked split open, revealing an eye full of tears. No matter where on the tree she took the fruit from, it always had an eye in it.

Finally, the woman realized it was useless. She climbed down from the tree, gathered up her pots, and returned home, weeping bitterly. She spent the rest of her days in sadness and mourning, and never again did she try to get her children back from the sycamore tree.

Part IV: The Influence of Isla

The Story of a Wager *(Tigre, Eritrea)*

The Tigre people of Eritrea are pastoralist nomads who embrace Islam. Arab influence in this EastAfrican country may be seen in the story retold below, which features the character Abunawas. Unlike the characters in most other folktales, Abunawas (d. 814) actually was a historical personage and one of the great poets of Arabic classical literature. Having a reputation that was somewhat larger than life, Abunawas eventually was fictionalized as a trickster character appearing in Arabic folklore including the Arabian Nights collection and many other stories.

Islamic conquerors and Arab traders brought these stories with them when they invaded the eastern coast of Africa, and so the stories worked their way into the folktale repertoire of the African peoples who converted to Islam. Abunawas' role in these tales usually involves tricking greedy, well-off people and showing them the error of their ways, which he does with a great deal of flair in the story retold below.

Once there were two men who made a wager. The first man said to the second, "I will give you all of my cattle if you can stay in the ocean all night long. But if you get out of the water before dawn, you have to give me all of your cattle."

The second said, "I accept your wager."

The second man soon realized that he had acted very foolishly. He thought about what he would have to do and became very frightened. He was sure he would fail and that he would lose all his cattle. He decided to go and ask an old woman he knew to be very wise. He told the woman about the wager and what he had to do, then he said, "Do you know how I might win this bet?"

"Yes, I do," she said. "Ask one of your relatives to go to the seashore with you. They are to build a fire on the beach across from where you will be. They must not let the fire go out at all. While you are in the water, keep your eyes fixed on the flames. That way you will feel warm and will be able to win your wager."

On the night that had been fixed for the wager, the second man and his mother went down to the beach. The mother made a fire, and then the man swam out until he was in deep water and could not touch the bottom. The first man hired watchmen to stand on the beach as well, to make sure that the second man did not come out of the water before daybreak.

And so the night passed, with the second man in the deep water with only his head above the surface, while his mother tended the fire on the beach and the watchmen stood by waiting to see whether the man would come ashore early. When the sun began to rise, the man swam back to the beach and came out of the water. He went to the first man and said, "I have won our wager. I spent the whole night in the ocean and came out alive."

"You have not won anything," said the first man. "My watchmen told me what happened. You were in the water looking at that fire all night. That's how you stayed warm and didn't die."

"How could I have kept warm?" said the second man. "I was so far away from the fire that its heat never reached me at all. Now give me all of your cattle, for I have won our wager."

But the people who were listening to the men agreed that because the second man had been looking at the fire, he hadn't won the bet.

"This will not do," said the second man. "If you will not pay me what you owe, I shall take our case before a judge."

"That is fine with me," said the first man, and so they went before a judge and told him their tale.

When the men were each done telling their side of the story, the judge said, "I find that the wager has been lost, because the man who was in the water looked at the fire all night."

The first man went home happy because he got to keep all of his cattle, but the second was crestfallen. Giving up all of his cattle would mean being ruined forever.

Finally, the second man had an idea. He went to Abunawas, who was a very clever man and had gotten out of many bad situations before. The man told Abunawas his story and how the judge had sided with the first man.

"I know just what to do," said Abunawas. Abunawas sent a messenger throughout the land, inviting everyone to a feast. The first man who had made the wager was invited, and the judge, and the people who had agreed with the first man, and many more besides. Everyone waited impatiently for the feast, for the messenger had told them it would be particularly good.

The day of the feast came, and Abunawas set his servants about slaughtering cattle and goats to make roast meats and stews and making huge pots of rice. But Abunawas said, "You shall not give any of this food to my guests until I tell you to, not even the smallest grain of rice or the smallest piece of meat."

The people came to the feast at the appointed time, and sat down outside Abunawas' house, waiting for the feast to start. Abunawas himself, however, stayed inside his house and said not a word. The servants, meanwhile, set out the food for the guests but did not begin to serve them. The people could see the good food, and smell it, and they said, "Why is Abunawas not serving the food? What kind of feast is this?"

A long time passed. The people became very hungry. But still the servants did not bring them their food. Finally, when the sun was about to set, the people asked one man whom they knew to be a friend of Abunawas to go inside and ask why the feast was not starting.

The friend went inside and said, "Your guests have been waiting all day. They wonder why they have not been served the feast. What shall I tell them?"

Abunawas said, "Go to the people and say, 'You have been smelling the roast meats and the stews and the rice all day, and you have seen them spread out on the table. Surely that should be enough to satisfy you.'"

The friend went back outside and told the people what Abunawas had said. The people became very angry and said, "That makes no sense. How can we be satisfied by food that is far away from us? How does the scent of cooked food satisfy us? How does the sight of cooked food satisfy us?"

Then Abunawas came out of the house and said, "Now you understand that just being able to see or smell something isn't the same as having it. If you can't satisfy your hunger by seeing or smelling cooked food, then neither could the man who spent the night in the sea have been kept warm by looking at a fire that was on the beach."

The people realized that Abunawas was right, and they made the first man pay his debt. When that was done, Abunawas served the feast to all of the people, and when the feast was over, they all went home.

And so it was that Abunawas used his cleverness to help the second man get the payment he was due for winning the wager.

Dschemil and Dschemila *(Berber, Libya)*

"Berber" is not the name of a particular culture but rather is an umbrella term for a group of closely related cultures from North Africa. While most Berbers live in settlements and practice agriculture, some groups, such as the Tuareg, are primarily nomadic. For the most part, Berbers practice Islam, although there is a small Jewish community as well.

In his edition of this story, author and folklorist Andrew Lang notes that he took it from a collection by German linguist Hans Stumme, who collected this and other stories in 1897 in the area around Tripoli. Stumme relied on two informants, one a 45-year-old man named Sidi Brahim ben Xali et-Tekbali, and the other a 15-year-old boy named Mhemmed ben Zumxa Brengali.

This tale follows arcs typical of fairy tales in many cultures. An evil man-eating ogre captures a young woman and turns her into his servant, then the young woman's betrothed comes to rescue her from the ogre's castle, which stands in a remote part of the desert, far from any human habitation. The young people manage to get away using magical objects the young woman steals from her captor. Although the young man struggles somewhat with some of the incidents that follow their escape, he eventually proves his love for his betrothed by honoring her fear that she will be recaptured and doing what is necessary to keep her safe, even if it goes against the traditions of their people.

Once there was a man named Dschemil, and he had a cousin named Dschemila. They had been promised to one another in marriage since they were very small children, but now that they were grown, Dschemil decided that it was time for them to wed. Dschemil, therefore, went to the nearest town to buy furnishings for their new house. The nearest town was quite far away; it took two or three days to get there and another two or three days to come back.

While Dschemil was away, Dschemila and her friends went out to gather firewood. As she picked up sticks, Dschemila came across an iron mortar lying on the ground. She picked it up and fastened it to the top of her bundle, but every time she tried to pick up the bundle to carry it, the mortar fell to the ground. Dschemila undid her bundle to put the mortar in the middle.

Just as Dschemila began to tie up her bundle again, her friends said, "Whatever are you doing over there? It's getting dark, and we're not going to wait for you."

"That's all right," said Dschemila. "You go on ahead. I want to keep this iron mortar I've found. I'll head home as soon as I have it tied up properly in my bundle."

"Very well," said the other young women, who then returned home.

As Dschemila worked to tie up the mortar in her bundle, the sun set. When the last ray of sunlight had gone below the horizon, the iron mortar transformed into a huge ogre. The ogre picked Dschemila up and carried her far, far away to his castle, a whole month's journey from Dschemila's village.

The ogre put Dschemila in a chamber of his castle and said, "Do not be afraid. You will not be harmed." Then the ogre went out, leaving Dschemila sitting in the chamber weeping bitter tears and shivering with fright.

When the other young women of the village returned home, Dschemila's mother noticed that her daughter was not among them.

"Where has my daughter gone?" said the mother. "Why did she not return with you?"

"She found an iron mortar and wanted to tie it up properly to bring it home," said the others. "We expect she'll be back soon."

Dschemila's mother hurried toward the forest to look for her daughter, calling her name all the while. The other villagers saw her and said, "Why don't you go back home? You're just one old woman; this is a job that strong men should be doing."

"Yes, I would welcome help," said the old woman, "but I am coming with you whether you like it or not. My daughter very likely is dead. She probably was bitten by an asp or maybe eaten by a lion."

Once the men understood that the old woman would not stay home, they let her come with them, and together they set out for the forest, taking with them one of the other young women to show where she had last seen Dschemila.

Soon they arrived at the place where Dschemila had been. There they found her bundle of sticks, but no trace of the young woman was to be seen anywhere. They called and called her name, but no one answered.

One of the men said, "Let's light a fire. She will be able to see it even from far away, and then she will know we are looking for her."

The others agreed that this was a good idea, and that while that man kindled the fire, the others should go off in different directions to see whether they could find the girl. They searched and searched all through the night, but they found nothing. When the sun rose, the men said to Dschemila's mother, "We can't find her. We should just go home. Your daughter probably ran off with some man or other."

"Yes, let us go home," said the old woman, "but first I would like to look in the river. Maybe someone threw her in there."

They went and looked in the river, but there was no sign of Dschemila. They all returned home, weary and crestfallen.

Dschemila's mother and father waited anxiously for four days for any news of their daughter, but none ever came. At the end of the fourth day, Dschemila's mother said, "Dschemil will be coming home soon. What are we to tell him?"

"We will tell him she is dead," said the father.

"He will ask to see the grave, and then he will know that something is amiss."

"Tomorrow we will slaughter a goat," said the father. "We will bury its head in the burial ground. We will bring Dschemil there and tell him that that is Dschemila's grave."

The next day, Dschemil arrived with a wagon full of beautiful carpets and cushions to show his bride. He went straight to his in-laws' house, but no sooner had he crossed the threshold than Dschemila's father said, "Greetings. Dschemila is dead."

The young man began to wail and weep. For a long time, he could do nothing else, and he could not speak. When he finally regained his senses, he asked, "Where have you buried her? Please take me to her grave."

The father brought Dschemil to the place where they had buried the goat's head. Dschemil brought along some of the beautiful things he had bought for the new house. He laid them down upon the freshly covered grave and began to weep and mourn. When night fell, he took all the things back to his home, and when day broke, he went back, bringing the things and his flute with him. For six months, he went every day to sit upon what he thought was Dschemila's grave with some of the gifts he had intended to give her, alternately weeping with grief and playing soft, mournful tunes on his flute.

At the time when Dschemil had given himself up to grief, a man was wandering through the desert. The sun was very hot, and the man had run out of water and was very thirsty. He saw before him a great castle, and thought that if only he could rest in the shade, he might find the strength to beg a little water from whoever lived there. He went up to the wall of the castle on the shaded side and sat down to take his ease. It was so lovely and cool in the shade of the castle that he nearly fell asleep, but he startled awake when he heard a soft voice saying, "Who are you? Are you a ghost or a living man?"

The man looked up and saw a girl leaning out of a window.

"I am a man," he said, "and likely a better one than your father or grandfather."

"I wish you good luck," she replied, "but why are you here? This is a land of ogres and all manner of horrible things."

"Is this really the home of an ogre?" asked the man.

"Oh, yes," said the girl. "And as soon as the sun sets, he will come home. If he finds you here, he will turn you into his supper. You need to leave at once, for the day is already getting old."

"I will not get far if I leave without having something to drink," said the man. "I have been journeying all day in the hot desert sun, and I am so thirsty! Please give me some water."

"I can't do that," said the girl, "but if you travel in that direction, you might find a well or a spring. The ogre always goes that way when he wants to get water for the castle."

The man stood up and began to walk away, but the girl called out, "Wait! Tell me where you are going."

"Why do you need to know that?" said the man.

"I have a favor to ask, if you're willing to do it, but I need to know which way you are going."

"I'm going to Damascus," said the man.

"Here is the favor: on your way, you will pass through my village. Ask for a man called Dschemil. Tell him, 'Dschemila is alive and waits for you. She is held captive in a castle out in the desert. Be of good courage.'"

The man promised to take her message, and he walked off in the direction she had shown him. Soon enough, he came across a spring of cool, clear water. The man knelt down and drank and drank until his thirst was quenched. Then he lay down near the spring and slept for a while.

When the man woke up, he said, "That maiden surely did right by me when she told me the way to this spring. I'd be dead if it wasn't for her. I will surely look for her village and take her message to Dschemil."

The man traveled for a whole month, asking at every village he passed through whether there was a man named Dschemil, but everyone always told him there was no one in their village with that name. At the end of that month, the man came to another village. He entered and saw a man sitting in front of one of the houses. The man's hair was long and unkempt, and his beard was shaggy. As the man walked toward the house, the unkempt man said, "Welcome to our village. Where have you come from?"

"I came from the west, and I am walking to the east," said the traveler.

"Come in and take supper with us," said the unkempt man. "You have had a long journey, and you must be hungry."

The traveler went inside, and was made welcome by Dschemila's parents and Dschemil's brothers, who set a meal on the table. All gathered around to eat, and they invited the traveler to partake with them. However, the traveler noticed that one member of the family was missing.

"Where is the unkempt man who invited me into your gracious home?" asked the traveler. "Will he not also eat with us?"

"Don't mind him," whispered one of Dschemil's brothers. "He does that every night. He'll eat something in the morning."

The traveler went on with his meal, wondering what was wrong with the shaggy man. Suddenly one of Dschemil's brothers called out, "Dschemil! Do go and get us some water, if you would."

When the traveler heard the name "Dschemil," he remembered what he had promised the young woman in the castle. "Dschemil!" said the traveler. "Does someone here have that name? I got lost in the desert and came across a castle. There was a maiden in the castle, and she looked out the window and said—"

"Shh!" said one of the brothers. "Don't let him hear you!"

But it was too late. The unkempt man came to the table and said, "Tell me all your tale. Tell me what you saw and what she said. Do it now, or I shall kill you right here."

"I will tell you all, sir," said the traveler. "I was lost in the desert, and before me I saw a castle. I thought to rest in its shade before carrying on with my journey. While I sat with my back against the castle wall, a maiden put her head out of a window above me and asked whether I was man or ghost. I told her I was a man and asked her whether she might give me a drink, for I was very thirsty. She said she had no water to give me, but told me of a spring that was not far off. She also warned me that I needed to leave straight away, for the castle is home to a horrible ogre who might eat me for his supper.

"Before I left, she asked which way I was going. I told her, and she asked a favor of me. She said that I was to find her village and to find the man named Dschemil who lived there, and that when I found him, I was to tell him, 'Dschemila is alive and waits for you. She is held captive in a castle out in the desert. Be of good courage.'"

For a long moment there was silence.

Then the unkempt man, who was indeed Dschemil, said, "Is this true? Is my beloved really still alive?"

The whole family protested that Dschemila was really dead and that the grave was indeed hers.

"We'll see whether you're telling the truth or not," said Dschemil. He snatched up a spade and made to leave for the burial ground.

"Wait!" cried Dschemila's parents. "We'll tell you the truth. Dschemila went out to gather firewood but didn't return with the others. When night fell, we went looking for her, but we couldn't find her anywhere, and she didn't come home. After four days, we decided the best thing to do would be to just tell you that she was dead and make a false grave to convince you that it was true. But since now you know the truth, you should go and find her. Perhaps this man will go with you as a guide; he has been to the castle, and he will be able to show you the way there."

"Yes," said the Dschemil, "that is the best way. Prepare food for my journey while I get my sword."

"Wait," said the traveler. "I don't want to go with you. It took me a whole month to get here, and I have more of my journey left to go, and that's a long way, too."

Dschemil said, "Please come with me for three days to set me on the right path. And after three days, we can each go our separate ways."

"That seems fair," said the traveler, and so they set out on their journey.

For three days Dschemil and his companion traveled from daybreak to dusk, and at dusk of the third day, the traveler said, "Go that way, and walk straight on until you come to a spring. Then keep going in the same direction, and soon enough you will see the castle."

"Very well," said Dschemil. Then the two men said their farewells and parted ways.

Dschemil journeyed on for twenty-six days, and on the evening of the twenty-sixth day, he came across the spring. "This must be the spring the traveler told me about," he said, then he knelt down to take a long drink of the clear, fresh water. When his thirst was quenched, he lay down beside the spring and thought about what he should do next.

"If this is the spring," he thought, "then the castle must be close by. The best thing I can do now is rest, and travel on to the castle in the morning."

And so Dschemil went to sleep there by the spring and slept long and peacefully all night.

Late the next morning, Dschemil awoke. He took another long drink from the spring, then set out to find the castle. It did not take long before he saw it rising out of the desert sand in front of him. "Now to figure out how to get in," Dschemil said. "I can't just knock at the door; surely if I do that, the ogre will grab me and eat me for supper."

Dschemil thought for a while more, then decided the best thing to do would be to climb the wall where maybe he could peep in through a window. He crept up to the castle and began to climb the wall, but no sooner had he arrived at the top than he heard a young woman's voice call out from above him, saying, "Dschemil!"

Dschemil looked up, and what should he see but his beloved Dschemila peeping out of a window above him! Dschemil began to weep for joy.

"My dear beloved one," said the girl, "what brings you here?"

"I came looking for you," he said.

"Oh, no," said Dschemila, "you mustn't. You must leave at once. If the ogre comes home and finds you here, he will kill and eat you!"

"I don't care if there are fifty ogres in this castle," said Dschemil. "I have not grieved for so long and traveled so far just to lose you again."

"If I lowered a rope to you," said Dschemila, "could you use it to climb up and come in through the window?"

"Certainly," the young man replied.

The young woman went back into her chamber. Soon enough, a light rope came down from the window. Dschemil took hold of the rope. He climbed up the rope and went in through the window. When he arrived in Dschemila's chamber, the two young lovers embraced one another tenderly and wept for joy.

"What will we do when the ogre comes back?" asked Dschemila.

"I have a plan," said Dschemil. "Trust me."

Now, Dschemila had a large chest in her chamber, where she kept her clothing and some other things. She had Dschemil get into the chest, and she closed the lid. No sooner had she closed the lid than the ogre came into the chamber, carrying a leg of lamb for Dschemila and two human legs for himself.

"I smell the smell of a man!" roared the ogre. "Where is he?"

"I don't know what you're talking about," said Dschemila. "We're out here in the middle of the desert. There's no one around for miles and miles. How could a man possibly get in here?" Then she burst into tears.

"Oh, my," said the ogre, "I did not mean to upset you. I must be mistaken. Perhaps a raven found some carrion and dropped scraps nearby."

"Yes, that's what happened," said Dschemila. "A raven dropped some bones the other day. I had forgotten."

"That's all right, then," said the ogre. "Go and fetch the bones and burn them into dust. Then put the powder in a cup of water that I may drink them. Bring it to me in the kitchen. You must cook supper for both of us."

Dschemila found some bones, burned them until they turned to dust, then put the powder into a cup of water. She gave this to the ogre, and he drank it. Then he lay down to sleep while Dschemila cooked.

After a little while, the man's legs that were roasting over the fire began to sing,

Ogre, do not rest!

A man is in the chest!

The leg of lamb answered,

That man is your brother

And cousin to this other

The ogre said sleepily, "Who is singing? What did they say?"

"It was only a reminder to add some salt to our dinners," said Dschemila.

"Well, add some salt, then."

"I've already done so."

Then the ogre rolled over and went back to sleep.

No sooner had the ogre fallen back to sleep than the man's legs began to sing,

Ogre, Ogre, do not rest!

A man is in the chest!

The leg of lamb answered,

That man is your brother

And cousin to this other

Again the ogre asked what the voices were saying.

"I need to add pepper this time," said Dschemila.

"Add the pepper, then," said the ogre.

"I've already done so."

The ogre was so very tired that he rolled over and went right back to sleep. A third time the man's legs began to sing.

Ogre, do not rest!

A man is in the chest!

The leg of lamb answered,

That man is your brother

And cousin to this other.

Again the ogre was roused from his sleep. "What did it say this time?" said the ogre.

"It says that it's ready for us to eat."

"Oh, good," said the ogre. "I am very hungry. Please serve me my food."

Dschemila fed the man's legs to the ogre and sliced up the lamb for herself, cleverly hiding some away to give to Dschemil later.

When the ogre finished eating, he washed his hands and then told Dschemila to go to his chamber and make up his bed for him. Dschemila did so, turning down the covers and plumping the pillow for him. The ogre got into bed, and Dschemila tucked him in. Then Dschemila asked, "Father, why do you always sleep with your eyes open?"

The ogre frowned. "Why do you ask? Are you thinking of doing something you shouldn't?"

"Oh, no!" said Dschemila, "I would never do that. I wouldn't even know where to begin, and surely I wouldn't succeed."

"All right, then, but why do you want to know?"

"Well," said Dschemila, "last night I happened to wake up in the middle of the night. The whole castle was shining with a red light. It frightened me, so I wanted to know where that came from and whether you saw it, too."

The ogre chuckled, "Oh, my child, you needn't be afraid of that. The red light happens when I am fast asleep."

"Oh, good," said Dschemila. "I'm glad that that's nothing that could hurt us. But may I ask what is the pin for, the one that you keep next to your bed?"

"The pin turns into an iron mountain if I throw it in front of me."

"Does the darning needle do anything special?"

"Why, yes," said the ogre. "It turns into a big lake."

"What about your hatchet?" said Dschemila.

"The hatchet becomes a thorn hedge so thick and with such long thorns that no one could hope to push through it." The ogre's eyes narrowed, and he looked at Dschemila suspiciously. "But why are you asking me all these questions? It makes me think you are up to no good, and that would make me very angry."

"I only wanted to know what they are for. I see them here all the time, but you never seem to use them. And anyway, where would I go? Who would ever find me here out in the middle of the desert?" And then Dschemila began to cry.

"Please don't cry," said the ogre. "I was only teasing."

"All right," said Dschemila, wiping away her tears. "I'll go to my own bed now. Good night, Father."

"Good night."

Dschemila went back into her chamber and closed the door. She let Dschemil out of the chest.

"Let's go!" said Dschemil. "Let's get out of here now!"

"No, wait," said Dschemila, who went to the door and opened it just a crack. "Do you see that yellow light? It means the ogre isn't asleep yet."

Dschemil and Dschemila waited for an hour. Then Dschemila opened the door a little bit again. There was a red light all over everything. "Look!" she said. "That red light means the ogre is asleep. How shall we escape?"

Dschemil said, "We'll use the rope you let down to me. I'll let you down first, then I'll follow."

"Yes, that is a good plan," said Dschemil. "You get the rope ready. I'm going to get some other things that could help us.

While Dschemil readied the rope, Dschemila crept back into the ogre's bedchamber. She silently took the pin, the darning needle, and the hatchet, and then ran as quickly as she dared back to her chamber. She handed the items to Dschemil and said, "Put these in your pockets. Be careful not to lose them. We may need them later."

"Very well," said Dschemil. Then he tied the rope around Dschemila and let her down. When she was safely on the ground, she untied the rope, and Dschemil used it to climb down himself. Then they both ran away from the castle as fast as they could go.

Now, the ogre slept all through this. He heard nothing when Dschemila came into his chamber and took his things. He heard nothing when the two lovers climbed down the wall. But the ogre had a faithful dog who discovered that Dschemila had escaped. He ran into the ogre's chamber and said, "Why are you sleeping? Dschemila has escaped, and she's running away."

For answer, the ogre kicked the dog, rolled over, and went back to sleep. In the morning, the ogre woke up and called for Dschemila as he usually did, but there was no answer. The ogre went up to Dschemila's chamber and found it empty. He roared with anger, then went downstairs, put on his armor, and picked up his sword. He called his dog and then went out in pursuit of the two lovers.

As Dschemil and Dschemila ran, Dschemila checked over her shoulder every once in a while to see whether the ogre was following them. For a long time, she saw nothing, but soon after daybreak, she looked back and, in the distance, saw the ogre and his dog in hot pursuit.

"The ogre is chasing us!" said Dschemila.

Dschemil looked back and said, "I don't see anything."

"He's there, in the distance. He looks as small as a needle, and he has his dog with him."

The two lovers began to run even faster, but no matter how fast they ran, the ogre still gained on them. When he was nearly upon them, Dschemila said, "Give me the pin, quickly!"

Dschemil gave her the pin, which she threw behind her. Instantly a mountain made out of iron rose up between them and the ogre.

"No matter!" roared the ogre. "We will break this iron into little pieces, and then we will catch you!"

The sound of the ogre and his dog digging and striking at the iron filled the air as Dschemil and Dschemila redoubled their pace. Soon the ogre and his dog had broken through the mountain and once again were catching up to the lovers.

"Dschemil!" cried Dschemila. "Quickly, throw the hatchet behind you!"

Dschemil took the hatchet out of his pocket and threw it over his shoulder. Instantly a hedge made of thorns so thick that no one could ever get through it grew up behind them.

"I may not be able to get through this hedge," roared the ogre, "but I can tunnel underneath!"

The sound of his digging filled the air as the two lovers ran on and on. In what seemed like no time at all, the ogre and his dog were on the other side of the hedge and getting closer and closer to the two young people.

"Dschemil!" cried Dschemila. "Throw the darning needle!"

Dschemil took the darning needle out of his pocket and threw it over his shoulder. Instantly a great lake formed in between the young people and their pursuers.

"Do you think a little bit of water can stop me?" thundered the ogre. "My dog and I will drink this lake dry, and then we will have you!"

The ogre and his dog began to drink the water from the lake. Soon the dog had drunk so much that it burst and died. The ogre realized that he could not finish all the water by himself, so he called out, "Dschemila! May your head become that of a donkey! May your hair turn into a donkey's coat!"

Dschemil turned to look at his cousin and found a strange creature standing next to him. It was wearing Dschemila's clothes, but it had the head and the coat of a donkey, and in the place of hands and feet, it had hooves. Dschemil took a step back in horror and said, "You were never my cousin. You were a little donkey-creature the entire time!" Dschemil ran away from the creature and went back to his own village.

Dschemila wandered about the desert all alone for two days, weeping all the while. Meanwhile, Dschemil had nearly arrived back at his village. He couldn't stop thinking about what had happened. He began to feel ashamed of himself for having abandoned the donkey. "What if it really was Dschemila after all?" he thought. "What if the ogre's spell has worn off? I can't leave her alone in the desert."

Dschemil turned back in search of his cousin. After a time, he found her, still with a donkey's head and coat, perched on top of a rock and surrounded by wolves. Dschemil drove the wolves away and helped his cousin down from the rock.

"Well, that was close," said Dschemil. "Those wolves would have had you if I hadn't come along."

Dschemila glared at her cousin. "Those wolves wouldn't have been anywhere near me if you had just taken me home."

"I thought you were a witch!" said Dschemil. "You turned into a donkey, right before my eyes!"

"Yes, I turned into a donkey," said Dschemila, "because the ogre cast a spell on me!"

"What did you expect me to do?" said Dschemil. "What would everyone have said if I came home leading a half-woman, half-donkey and said, 'Behold, I have rescued Dschemila?'"

"What are you going to do now?" said Dschemila.

"I don't know."

"Why don't you take me home at night? Just bring me to my mother's house, and I'll do the rest."

They waited next to the rocks until the sun had set, then journeyed back to the village. When they arrived, they went to Dschemila's mother's house and knocked on the door.

"Who is there?" the mother said.

"It is I, Dschemil."

The mother opened the door, and Dschemil said, "I found Dschemila, and I've brought her home."

The mother looked at the little donkey and said, "Since when have I been the mother of a donkey? That is not my daughter. You need to leave right now. This is foolishness."

"Hush!" said Dschemil. "Do you want to wake the whole village? This really is Dschemila. She's under a spell."

Dschemila sobbed. "Mother, it really is me. Do you not know me?"

"Do you remember that Dschemila had two scars?" said Dschemil.

"Yes, she had one on her thigh from a dog bite," said the mother, "and another on her breast from a burn with lamp oil that she got when she was small."

Dschemila took off her clothes and showed the two scars to her mother. When the mother saw that this indeed was her daughter, she embraced her joyfully, and they both wept. "Oh, daughter," said the mother, "who did this to you?"

"It was the ogre, Mother," said Dschemila. "He captured me when I was in the forest gathering firewood, and he kept me in his castle. Then Dschemil rescued me, but the ogre put a spell on me while we were escaping."

"I am very glad you are home and safe, but what are we going to tell everyone?" said the mother.

"Hide me here in your home," said Dschemila. "And Dschemil, if anyone asks whether you found me, keep pretending that I'm still lost. I'll take care of the rest."

The mother hid Dschemila in her home, and Dschemil returned to his family.

"Welcome home!" said Dschemil's father. "Did you find your cousin?"

"No, not a trace. I looked everywhere."

"What happened to the man who went with you?" said Dschemil's brother.

"After three days I had to let him leave. He was useless. He's probably arrived at his own home by now. I searched every castle I could find, but there was no sign of Dschemila anywhere."

"Ah, well," said Dschemil's father. "She probably got snatched by an ogre who ate her for his supper. Not much one can do about that."

Even after Dschemil repeated this story many times, people still kept asking him whether he was going to go look for Dschemila again, and every time he said he was not.

"All right then," said his friends and family, "we'll just have to find you someone else to be your wife. There are many beautiful girls in this village who would be pleased to marry you. Choose one."

But every time, Dschemil said he would have none other but his cousin. The people of the village began to think him mad. "You went out and bought all those furnishings, and now they're just sitting around unused. Choose another girl! Marry, and be happy!"

"I will never marry anyone other than my beloved Dschemila," said Dschemil. "Stop asking me!"

Three months went by. Then one day a merchant drew near to the ogre's castle. He went to sit in the shade of the wall, and the ogre found him there.

"What are you doing near my castle?" said the ogre.

The man stood up, trembling with fear.

"Please, sir, I am only a merchant. See? This is my bundle of goods. I sell clothing."

"Don't be afraid," said the ogre. "I won't eat you. At least not yet. I need your help."

"What do you want me to do?" said the merchant.

"Go in that direction," said the ogre, "and after a few days, you will come to a village. Take this comb and mirror, and ask the people of the village whether they know a young woman named Dschemila and a young man named Dschemil. When you find the young woman, give her the comb and the mirror and tell her, 'Your father the ogre bids you look in this mirror, and your own face will be returned to you. Then comb your coat with this comb, and all will be restored to you as it was before.'"

"I will do everything you say," said the merchant.

"That is good," said the ogre, "because if you don't, I will eat you for sure."

After a long journey, the merchant arrived at Dschemila's village. He sat down as soon as he could find a good spot, because he was tired, hungry, and very, very thirsty. Dschemil came upon him sitting there and said, "You really should get out of the sun. You will get sunstroke if you stay there."

"Yes, thank you," said the merchant, "but I have been traveling for a whole month, and I am too tired and hungry and thirsty to move right now."

"From where did you come?"

The merchant pointed in the direction of the ogre's castle. "That way," he said.

"Did you see anything interesting on your travels?" asked Dschemil.

"I did indeed. I came across a castle, and the ogre there told me to look for a young woman called Dschemila and a young man called Dschemil. Do those people live here?"

"I am Dschemil. What does the ogre want?"

"He gave me gifts to give to the young woman," said the merchant.

"Come with me," said Dschemil, and he led the merchant to his aunt and uncle's house.

When they arrived, Dschemila's mother asked, "Who is this man, and what does he want?"

"I am a merchant, ma'am, and I am looking for a young woman named Dschemila. An ogre sent me to look for her. He asked me to give her this comb and this mirror."

"It's a trick," said the mother. "Surely that ogre is only trying to harm my daughter further."

"I'm not sure that it's a trick," said Dschemil. "I think we should try."

Dschemila's mother called her daughter out of her hiding place and told her about the merchant. Dschemila went to the merchant and said, "I hear the ogre sent you with some things for me."

"Yes," said the merchant. "He sent me with this comb and this mirror, and he told me that I was to say that your father the ogre sent these to you, and that you were to look into the mirror and comb your coat with the comb, and that if you did that, you would become as you used to be."

Dschemila took the mirror and looked into it, and she combed her coat with the comb. When she was done, in place of a creature that looked like a donkey, there stood a beautiful young woman. Dschemila's mother and cousin rejoiced greatly to see the young woman restored. Soon word went through the village that Dschemila had returned. Everyone wanted to know when she got back, but all she would say was, "Dschemil brought me, but I didn't want to reveal myself right away. I wanted to wait until the time felt right."

Then Dschemil said to his parents and brothers and in-laws, "Let us have the wedding today. We have waited so long, but now Dschemila is here and we can be married."

The villagers prepared a beautiful litter to carry the bride to her new home, but Dschemila would not ride in it. "What if the ogre sees me?" she said. "Surely he will come and take me away again."

The men of the village said, "We wouldn't let him come near you. There are many of us, and we all have swords."

"It doesn't matter how many you are or how sharp your swords," said Dschemila. "That ogre is ruthless and cunning. I know him."

One old man said, "We should listen to her. If she won't ride the litter to her new house, maybe she can walk."

The others protested that the ogre couldn't possibly take her away again, but Dschemila would not be swayed. She would neither ride the litter nor walk. Soon it looked like an argument would break out, but Dschemil said, "If she is too afraid to leave this house, then I will live here with her. We can still have the wedding feast, and Dschemila will feel safe and cared for."

And so Dschemil and Dschemila were finally made man and wife, and they lived together in great peace and happiness to the end of their days.

Check out more mythology books by Matt Clayton

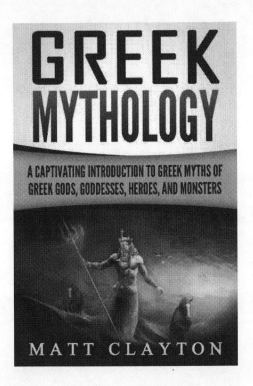

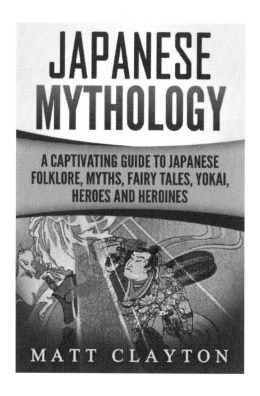

Bibliography

Barker, William Henry, and Cecilia Sinclair. *West African Folk-Tales*. London: G. G. Harrap & Company, 1917.

Bishop, Herbert L. "A Selection of SiRonga Folklore." *South African Journal of Science* 19 (1922): 383-400.

Callaway, Henry. *Nursery Tales, Traditions, and Histories of the Zulus, in their own Words*. Springvale, Natal: J. A. Blair, 1868.

Ceni, A. *African Folktales*. Trans. Elizabeth Leister. n. c.: Barnes & Noble, Inc., 1998.

Chatelain, Heli. *Folk-Tales of Angola*. Boston: Houghton Mifflin, 1894.

Cole, Joanna. *Best-Loved Folktales of the World*. Garden City: Doubleday & Company, 1982.

Courlander, Harold. *The Hat-Shaking Dance and Other Ashanti Tales from Ghana*. New York: Harcourt, Brace & World, Inc., 1957.

Dennett, R. E. *Notes on the Folklore of the Fjort (French Congo)*. Publications of the Folk-Lore Society, vol. 41. London: David Nutt, 1898.

Garner, Alan. *The Guizer: A Book of Fools*. New York: Greenwillow Books, 1976.

Lang, Andrew, ed. *The Grey Fairy Book*. London: Longmans, Green, and Co., 1905.

Lester, Julius. *How Many Spots Does a Leopard Have? and Other Tales*. New York: Scholastic, Inc., 1989.

———. *Black Folktales*. New York: Richard W. Baron, 1969.

Littman, Enno. *Publications of the Princeton Expedition to Abyssinia*. Vol. 2. Leyden: E. J. Brill, 1910.

Lynch, Patricia Ann. *African Mythology A to Z*. New York: Facts on File, Inc., 2004.

Mayo, Isa Fyvie. *Old Stories and Sayings of the Continent of Africa*. London: C. W. Daniel, n.d.

Radin, Paul, ed. *African Folktales*. Princeton: Princeton University Press, 1970.

Riley, Dorothy Winbush. *The Complete Kwanzaa: Celebrating our Cultural Harvest*. New York: HarperPerennial, 1995.

Scheub, Harold. *African Tales*. Madison: University of Wisconsin Press, 2005.

Stumme, Hans. *Märchen und Gedichte aus der Stadt Tripolis in Nordafrika*. Leipzig: J. C. Hinrichs'sche Buchhandlung, 1898.

Theall, George McCall. *Kaffir Folk-Lore*. London: Swan Sonnenschein, Le Bas & Lowrey, 1886.

Tremearne, A. J. N. *Hausa Superstitions and Customs: An Introduction to the Folk-Lore and the Folk.* London: J. Bale, Sons & Danielson, Ltd., 1913.

Tyler, Josiah. *Forty Years Among the Zulus.* Boston: Congregational Sunday-School and Pub. Society, 1891.

Made in United States
Orlando, FL
17 December 2023

41263452R00064